RAND McNALLY

W9-BMS-447

kids' road atlas

FUN!

Table of Contents

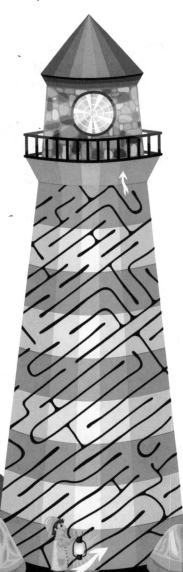

Using an Atlas...

Adventure or Mystery?

Is map reading an adventure or a mystery? It's only a mystery if you haven't uncovered the clues and codes. The information below will help you unlock the mystery and get started on the adventure. Solve the clues and use the numbered letters to fill in the secret message. For some of the clues you'll need to use the legend, scale, and coordinates, but for others you'll have to do a bit more detective work. Take a closer look at the maps for familiar cities, bordering states, and other details to help you find the answers. Good luck!

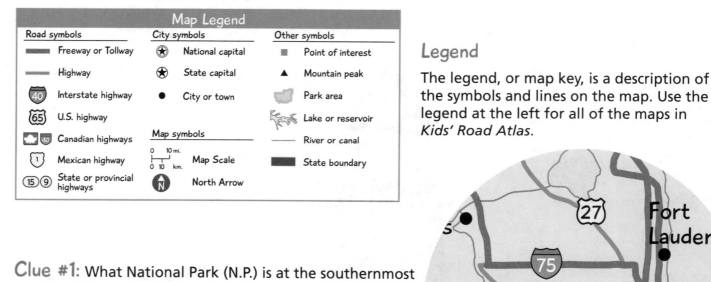

Legend

The legend, or map key, is a description of the symbols and lines on the map. Use the legend at the left for all of the maps in *Kids' Road Atlas*.

Clue #1: What National Park (N.P.) is at the southernmost section of the map at the right?

___ ___ ___ ___ ___ ___ ___ ___ ___ N.P.
         1   2

Clue #2: In what state will you find this park?

___ ___ ___ ___ ___ ___ ___
     3 4

Scale

Maps come in all sizes. Some show the whole world and others show only a small neighborhood. The map scale tells you how space on a map equals distance on the earth. Scale is used to measure distances between places on a map. Measure the length of the distance from place to place on the map and then use the scale to find out how many miles or kilometers that is. The maps in Kids' Road Atlas are not all at the same scale, so be sure to look at the scale on each map to measure distance correctly.

Clue #3: On the map at the right, what "mile-high" city is approximately 30 miles southeast of Boulder on Interstate 25?

___ ___ ___ ___ ___ ___
   5   6

Clue #4: In what state will you find these two cities?

___ ___ ___ ___ ___ ___ ___ ___
  7   8

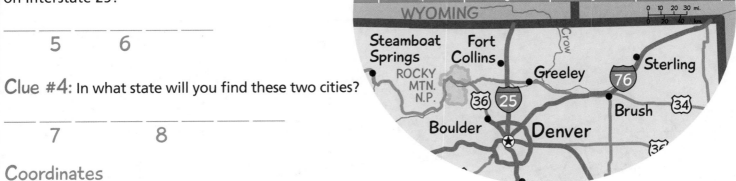

Coordinates

A coordinate is a letter–number combination that helps you find places on a map. To locate a city, look in the index to find the coordinate for that city. If, for example, the coordinate for the city is B–5, look down the right or left edge of the map for the letter B and draw an imaginary line across the map. Then, look across the top or bottom of the map for the number 5 and draw an imaginary line down or up until it meets the imaginary line drawn from the letter B. The city will be inside the area around this point. For each map in the *Kids' Road Atlas* there is an orange coordinate border with letters and numbers.

Clue #5: What coastal city on the map below is at coordinate H–5? Hint: There are several, so make sure you pick the one that fits in the blanks.

___ ___ ___ ___ ___ ___   ___ ___ ___   ___ ___ ___ ___
 9 10 11   12   13

Clue #6: In what state is this city located?

___ ___ ___ ___ ___ ___ ___ ___ ___ ___
        14   15

Clue #7: You'll find this Mexican city at coordinate I–5.

___ ___ ___ ___ ___ ___ ___
16   17   18

Have you solved all the clues? Congratulations! Use the letters from the numbered spaces in your answers to figure out this secret message:

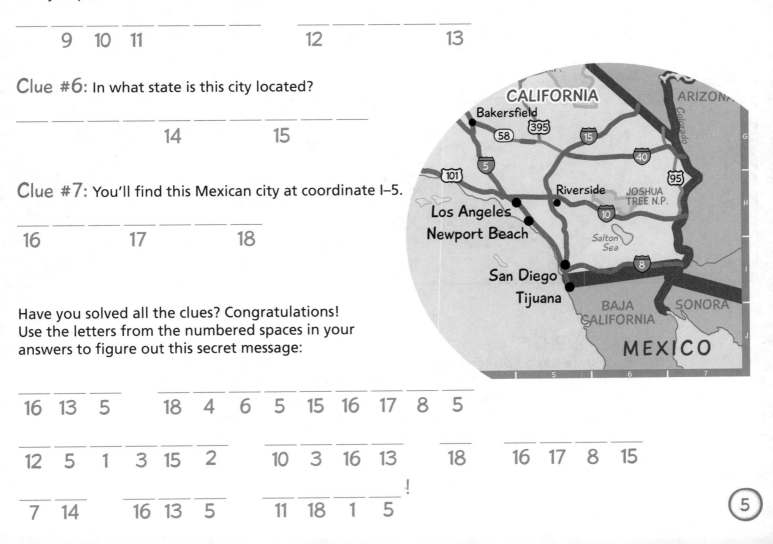

___ ___ ___   ___ ___ ___ ___ ___ ___ ___ ___ ___
16 13 5   18 4   6   5 15 16 17 8   5

___ ___ ___ ___ ___ ___   ___ ___ ___ ___   ___   ___ ___ ___ ___
12 5 1   3 15 2   10 3 16 13   18   16 17 8 15

___ ___   ___ ___ ___   ___ ___ ___ ___!
7 14   16 13 5   11 18 1   5

United States | Capital: Washington, D.C.

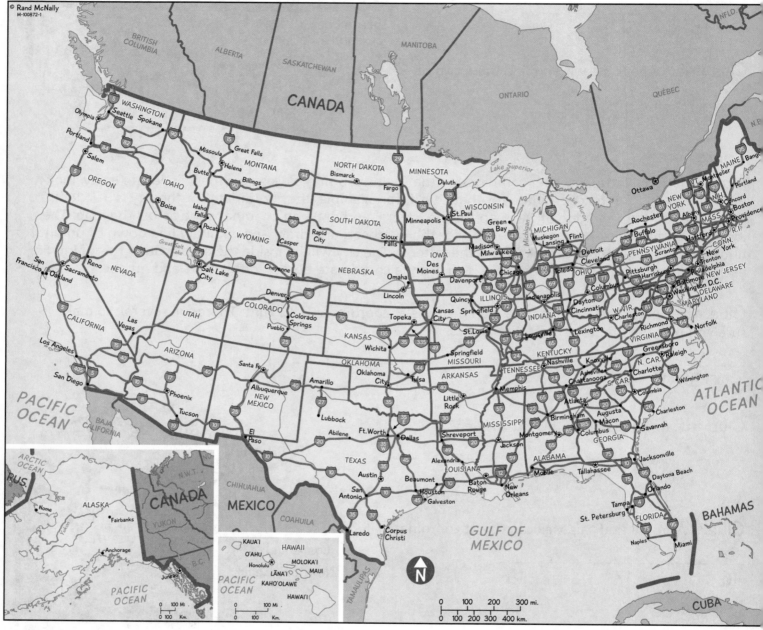

Keep it Brief

Each state has a two-letter abbreviation. On the next page, write the abbreviation for each state in the blanks provided. Remember that the two-letter abbreviation should be written in capital letters. Hint: Check out the state names in the red bar at the top of the pages in this book. The two letters of the abbreviation are the two capital letters in the name.

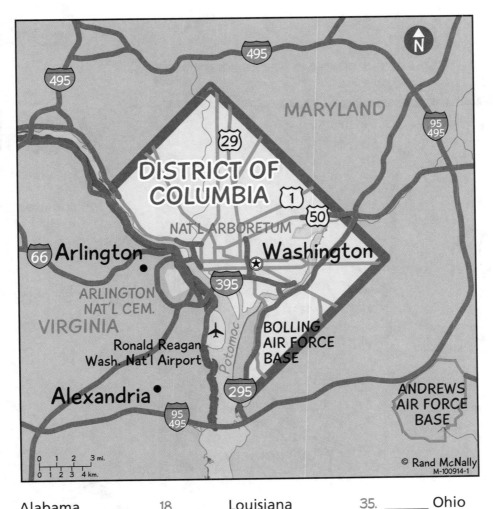

1. _____ Alabama

2. _____ Alaska

3. _____ Arizona

4. _____ Arkansas

5. _____ California

6. _____ Colorado

7. _____ Connecticut

8. _____ Delaware

9. _____ Florida

10. _____ Georgia

11. _____ Hawaii

12. _____ Idaho

13. _____ Illinois

14. _____ Indiana

15. _____ Iowa

16. _____ Kansas

17. _____ Kentucky

18. _____ Louisiana

19. _____ Maine

20. _____ Maryland

21. _____ Massachusetts

22. _____ Michigan

23. _____ Minnesota

24. _____ Mississippi

25. _____ Missouri

26. _____ Montana

27. _____ Nebraska

28. _____ Nevada

29. _____ New Hampshire

30. _____ New Jersey

31. _____ New Mexico

32. _____ New York

33. _____ North Carolina

34. _____ North Dakota

35. _____ Ohio

36. _____ Oklahoma

37. _____ Oregon

38. _____ Pennsylvania

39. _____ Rhode Island

40. _____ South Carolina

41. _____ South Dakota

42. _____ Tennessee

43. _____ Texas

44. _____ Utah

45. _____ Vermont

46. _____ Virginia

47. _____ Washington

48. _____ West Virginia

49. _____ Wisconsin

50. _____ Wyoming

ALabama

Southern pine | Camellia | Yellowhammer

BLaSt OFF!

Use the code to discover where the Space and Rocket Center is located. Write the correct letters in the blanks at the bottom of the page.

A B E H I L

M N S T U V

8

AlasKa

Nickname: The Last Frontier | **Capital:** Juneau

Sitka spruce | Forget-me-not | Willow ptarmigan

DiSCOVeriNG aLaSKa

Circle the Alaska words in the grid.

- ANCHORAGE
- BALD EAGLE
- DOG SLED RACE
- ESKIMO
- GLACIER
- GOLD
- GRIZZLY BEAR
- IGLOO
- JUNEAU
- KAYAK
- MOOSE
- MOUNTAIN
- OTTER
- SALMON
- SNOW
- TREE
- REINDEER
- TUNDRA
- WATERFALL
- WHALE

K	L	L	A	F	R	E	T	A	W	M	O
B	A	L	D	E	A	G	L	E	S	O	A
S	U	Y	L	T	R	E	E	N	L	O	N
R	A	E	A	T	D	L	O	G	O	S	C
E	E	L	S	K	N	W	I	L	M	E	H
E	N	G	M	O	U	N	T	A	I	N	O
D	U	O	T	O	T	O	A	C	K	L	R
N	J	A	S	K	N	T	A	I	S	S	A
I	O	O	W	H	A	L	E	E	E	N	G
E	D	O	G	S	L	E	D	R	A	C	E
R	A	E	B	Y	L	Z	Z	I	R	G	X

AriZona

Palo verde | Saguaro cactus blossom | Cactus wren

Map Labels

NEVADA · UTAH · COLORADO · NEW MEXICO · CALIFORNIA

15 · Page · Lake Powell · 160 · 191 · Lake Mead · Colorado · 89 · Hoover Dam · LAKE MEAD N.R.A. · GRAND CANYON N.P. · PETRIFIED FOREST N.P. · Kingman · Flagstaff · 40 · 93 · 89 · Prescott · ARIZONA · 17 · Springerville · 60 · 60 · 10 · Phoenix · Globe · 191 · 95 · Gila · 70 · 8 · 85 · 10 · SAGUARO N.P. · Yuma · Tucson · 10 · 19 · 191 · Nogales · SONORA · Douglas · Gulf of California · MEXICO

© Rand McNally
M-100856-1

MiGHTY GRAND

The Grand Canyon (C–2) is one of the seven natural wonders of the world. Its size is incredible! Solve the problems to find out just how big it is.

How Deep?

The Grand Canyon could fit this many Empire State Buildings inside its walls, stacked on top of one another!

$$\left[\begin{array}{c}\text{The number of the}\\\text{Interstate highway}\\\text{that runs east-west}\\\text{through Flagstaff}\end{array}\right] / \left[\begin{array}{c}\text{The number of the}\\\text{Interstate highway}\\\text{that runs east-west}\\\text{through Tuscon}\end{array}\right] =$$

——— = ———

How Long?

The Grand Canyon is this many miles long—almost the same as the width of the state of Utah!

$$\left[\begin{array}{c}\text{The number}\\\text{of the}\\\text{U.S highway}\\\text{that runs}\\\text{down}\\\text{Arizona's}\\\text{eastern}\\\text{border}\end{array}\right] + \left[\begin{array}{c}\text{The number}\\\text{of the}\\\text{state}\\\text{highway}\\\text{that}\\\text{runs from}\\\text{Globe to}\\\text{Springerville}\end{array}\right] - \left[\begin{array}{c}\text{The number}\\\text{of the}\\\text{Interstate}\\\text{highway}\\\text{running}\\\text{west from}\\\text{Phoenix}\end{array}\right] +$$

$$\left[\begin{array}{c}\text{The number of the}\\\text{Interstate highway}\\\text{that runs north}\\\text{from Phoenix}\end{array}\right] + \left[\begin{array}{c}\text{The number of the}\\\text{Interstate highway}\\\text{that runs from}\\\text{south from Tucson}\end{array}\right] =$$

——— = ———

ARkansas

Nickname: The Natural State | Capital: Little Rock

Pine | Apple blossom | Mockingbird

It's a road rally from Hot Springs (D–3) to where? When you race in a rally you are given a map with your beginning city only. Can you figure out which towns are on the route after Hot Springs? Use the map above to help fill in the blanks on the Road Rally Map.

CAlifornia

Nickname: The Golden State **Capital:** Sacramento

California redwood | Golden poppy | California (valley) quail

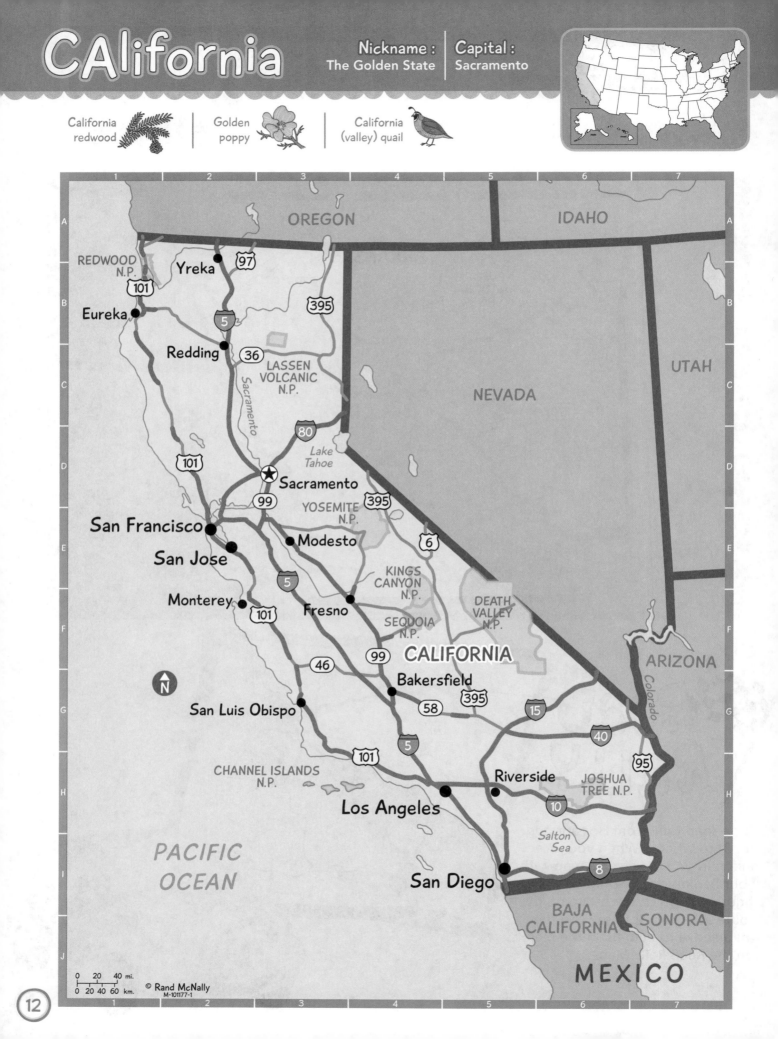

OREGON

IDAHO

REDWOOD N.P.

Yreka **97**

101

Eureka

5 **395**

Redding **36**

LASSEN VOLCANIC N.P.

Sacramento *(river)*

NEVADA

UTAH

80

Lake Tahoe

101

★ Sacramento

99 YOSEMITE N.P. **395**

San Francisco

Modesto **6**

San Jose

KINGS CANYON N.P.

5

Monterey Fresno

101

SEQUOIA N.P.

DEATH VALLEY N.P.

46 **99** CALIFORNIA

ARIZONA

Bakersfield

San Luis Obispo **58** **395**

Colorado *(river)*

5 **15**

101 **40**

CHANNEL ISLANDS N.P. **95**

Riverside JOSHUA TREE N.P.

Los Angeles **10**

Salton Sea

PACIFIC OCEAN

San Diego **8**

BAJA CALIFORNIA SONORA

MEXICO

N

0 20 40 mi.
0 20 40 60 km.

© Rand McNally
M-101177-1

12

Park it here

Look at the map of California for the National Parks that are located at the coordinates listed below. Write the names of the parks in the puzzle. The shaded column will spell out California's state motto, reading from top to bottom.

1. B–1
2. F–4
3. H–6
4. D–3
5. E–4
6. F–5

Colorado blue spruce | Columbine | Lark bunting

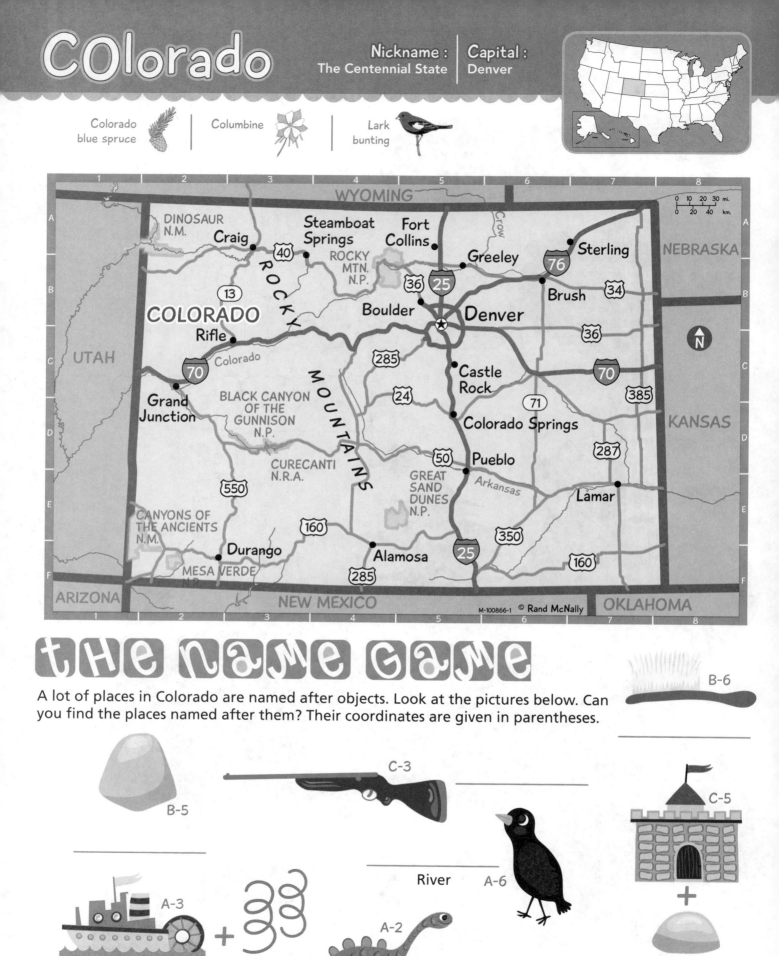

THe name Game

A lot of places in Colorado are named after objects. Look at the pictures below. Can you find the places named after them? Their coordinates are given in parentheses.

B-6

C-3

C-5

B-5

A-3

River   A-6

A-2

National Monument

ConnecTicut

Nickname: The Constitution State | Capital: Hartford

White oak | Mountain laurel | American robin

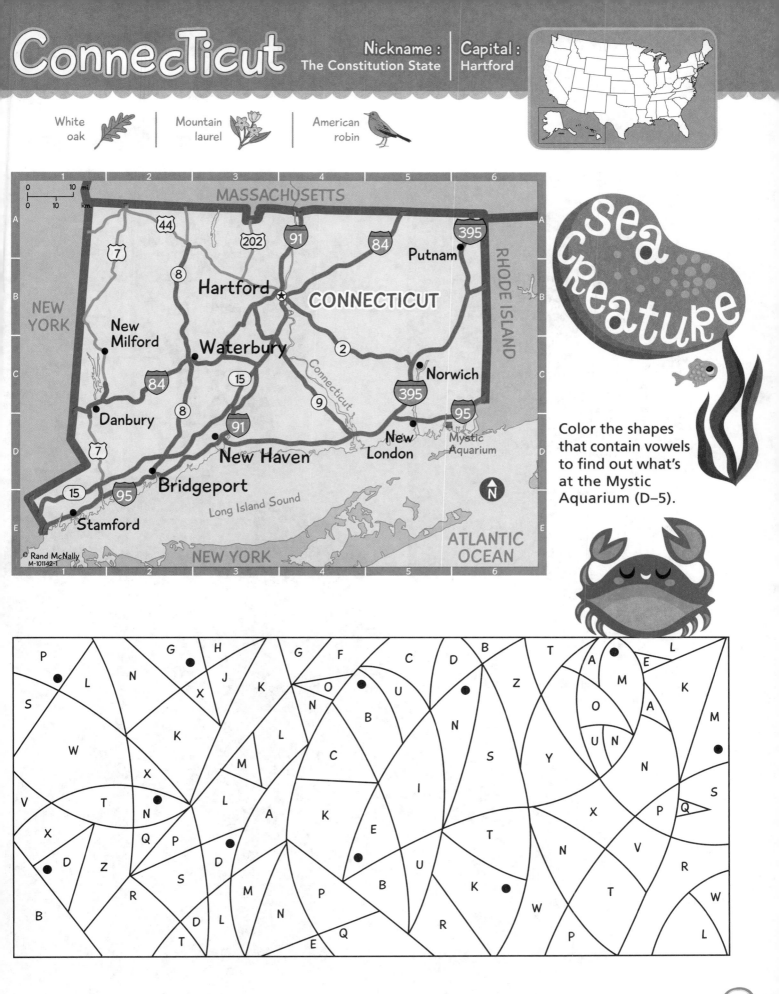

sea creature

Color the shapes that contain vowels to find out what's at the Mystic Aquarium (D–5).

DElaware

Nickname:
The First State

Capital:
Dover

American holly

Peach blossom

Blue hen chicken

© Rand McNally
M-101143-1

PENNSYLVANIA

95 Claymont
Newark
Wilmington
New Castle

NEW JERSEY

301

Middletown
1 Smyrna
13 **Dover**
8

Delaware Bay

DELAWARE

14 Milford
113
Rehoboth Beach
Georgetown 9
Seaford 1
Bethany Beach
13

MARYLAND

ATLANTIC OCEAN

0   10 mi.
0   10 km.

SHip Shape

Delaware is well-known for its maritime history. Can you spot the correct reflection for this ship?

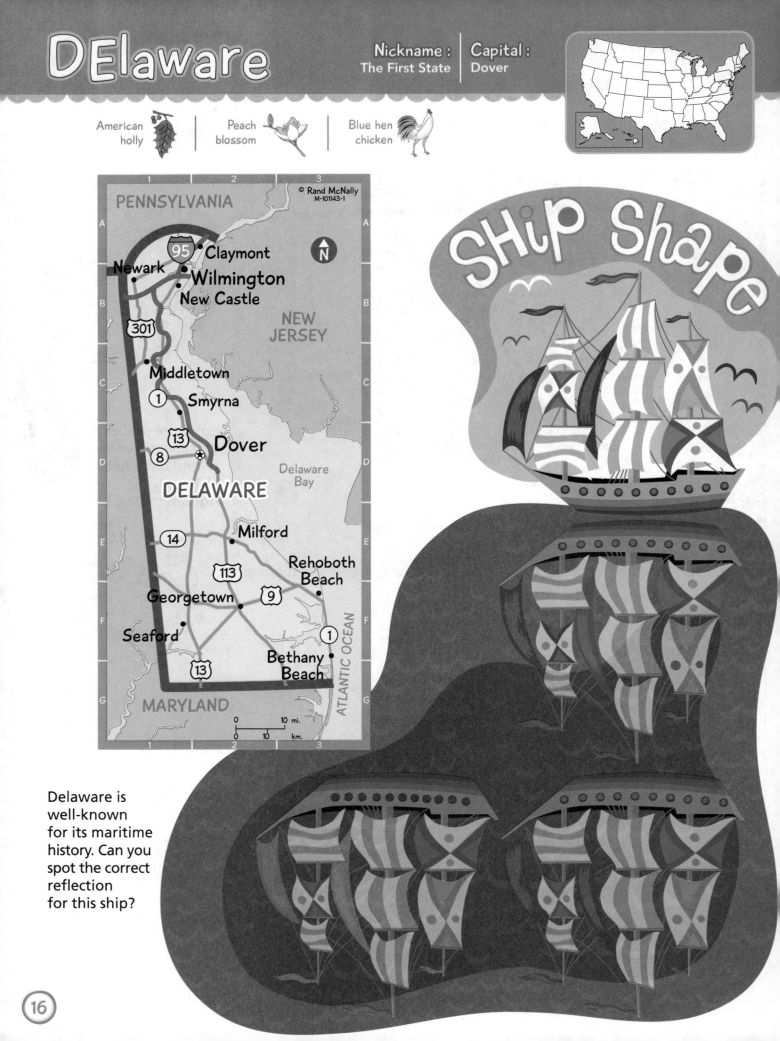

FLorida

Sabal palm | Orange blossom | Mockingbird

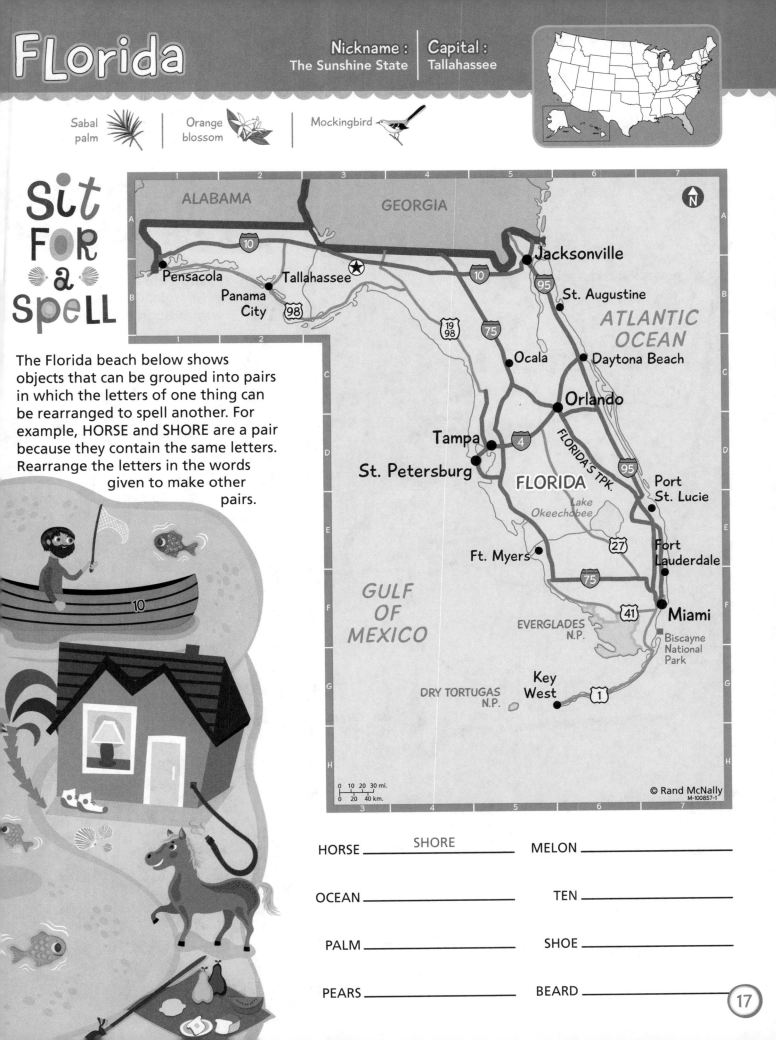

Sit FoR a SpeLL

The Florida beach below shows objects that can be grouped into pairs in which the letters of one thing can be rearranged to spell another. For example, HORSE and SHORE are a pair because they contain the same letters. Rearrange the letters in the words given to make other pairs.

HORSE __SHORE__   MELON _____

OCEAN _____   TEN _____

PALM _____   SHOE _____

PEARS _____   BEARD _____

GeorgiA

Nickname: The Peach State | Capital: Atlanta

Live oak | Cherokee rose | Brown thrasher

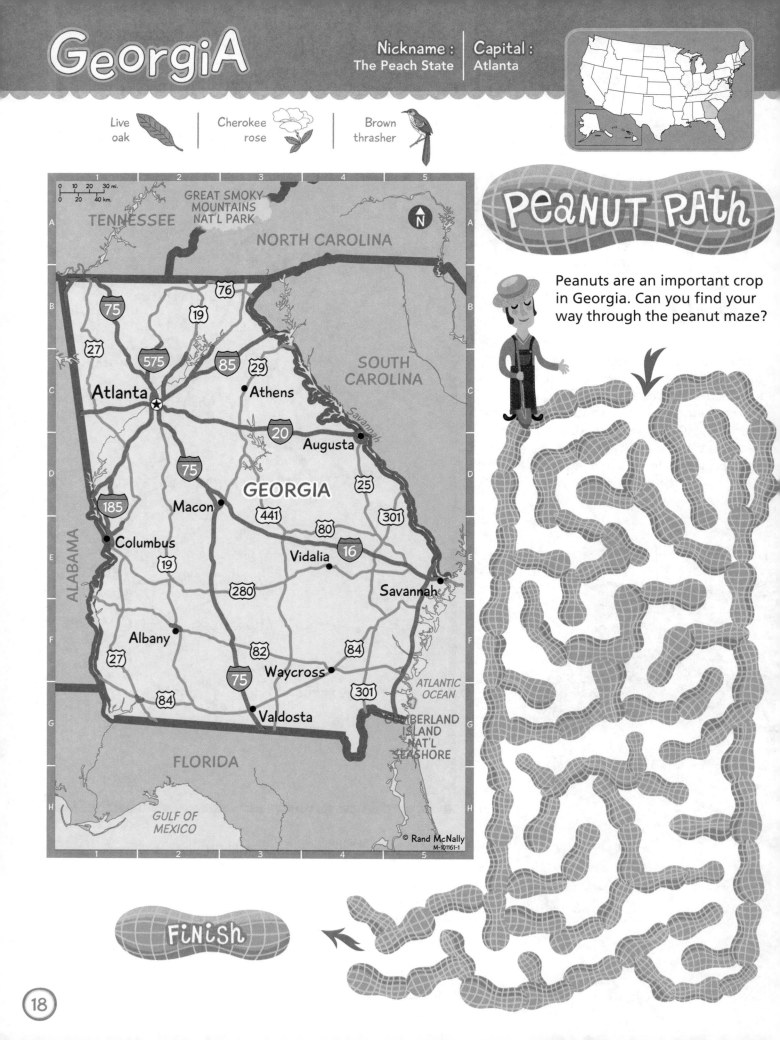

PEANUT PATH

Peanuts are an important crop in Georgia. Can you find your way through the peanut maze?

FiNish

Hawaii

Nickname: The Aloha State | Capital: Honolulu

Kukui (candlenut) | Yellow hibiscus | Nene (Hawaiian goose)

© Rand McNally
M-100878-1

Hanalei
KAUA'I
Kekaha
Lihu'e
56
NI'IHAU
Kauai Channel
O'AHU
83
Pearl City
Wai'anae
H1
★ Honolulu
Kaiwi Channel
MOLOKA'I
Kaunakakai
Wailuku
360
MAUI
Lāna'i City
HALEAKALĀ NAT'L PARK
LĀNA'I
KAHO'OLAWE
HAWAII
Alenuihaha Channel
Waimea
19
Hilo
200
Kailua
Mountain View
HAWAI'I
11
HAWAI'I VOLCANOES NAT'L PARK
PACIFIC OCEAN

N

0 10 20 30 mi.
0 20 40 km.

active Hawaii

Connect the dots to find out what Kilauea is. Kilauea is in the National Park at coordinate E–6.

IDaho

Western white pine | Syringa (mock orange) | Mountain bluebird

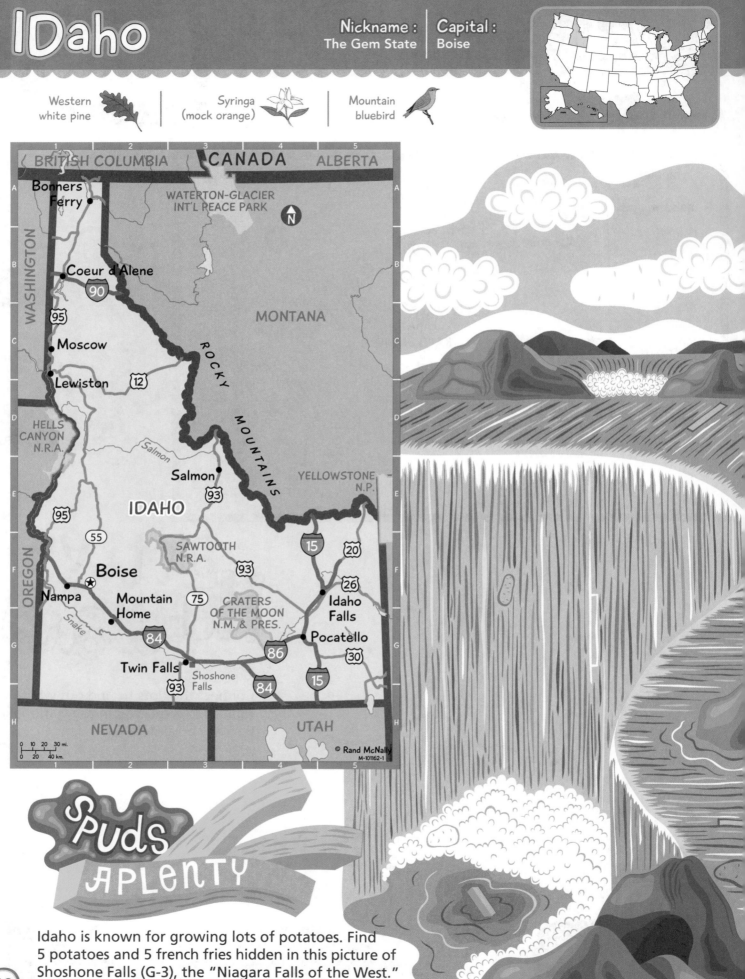

CANADA

BRITISH COLUMBIA | ALBERTA

WATERTON-GLACIER INT'L PEACE PARK

Bonners Ferry

WASHINGTON

Coeur d'Alene — 90

95

Moscow

Lewiston — 12

MONTANA

ROCKY MOUNTAINS

HELLS CANYON N.R.A.

Salmon

Salmon — 93

IDAHO

YELLOWSTONE N.P.

OREGON

95

55

SAWTOOTH N.R.A.

93

15 | 20

Boise — ★

Nampa

Mountain Home

75

Snake

84

CRATERS OF THE MOON N.M. & PRES.

26

Idaho Falls

Pocatello

30

Twin Falls — 93 — Shoshone Falls

86

84 | 15

NEVADA | UTAH

© Rand McNally
M-101162-1

0 10 20 30 mi.
0   20   40 km.

Spuds Aplenty

Idaho is known for growing lots of potatoes. Find 5 potatoes and 5 french fries hidden in this picture of Shoshone Falls (G-3), the "Niagara Falls of the West."

Illinois

Nickname: Land of Lincoln   **Capital:** Springfield

White oak | Native violet | Cardinal

tour of illinois

Follow the directions for a tour of Illinois. Write the names of the cities you visit as you go.

1. _____
A place to say "Bonjour." (E–5)

2. _____
A place for Santa Claus and Abraham Lincoln. (D–2)

3. _____
A place to have lunch. (B–4)

4. _____
A place to avoid. (B–3)

5. _____
A place to have an average time. (C–4)

6. _____
A place where a poor speller could celebrate. (D–4)

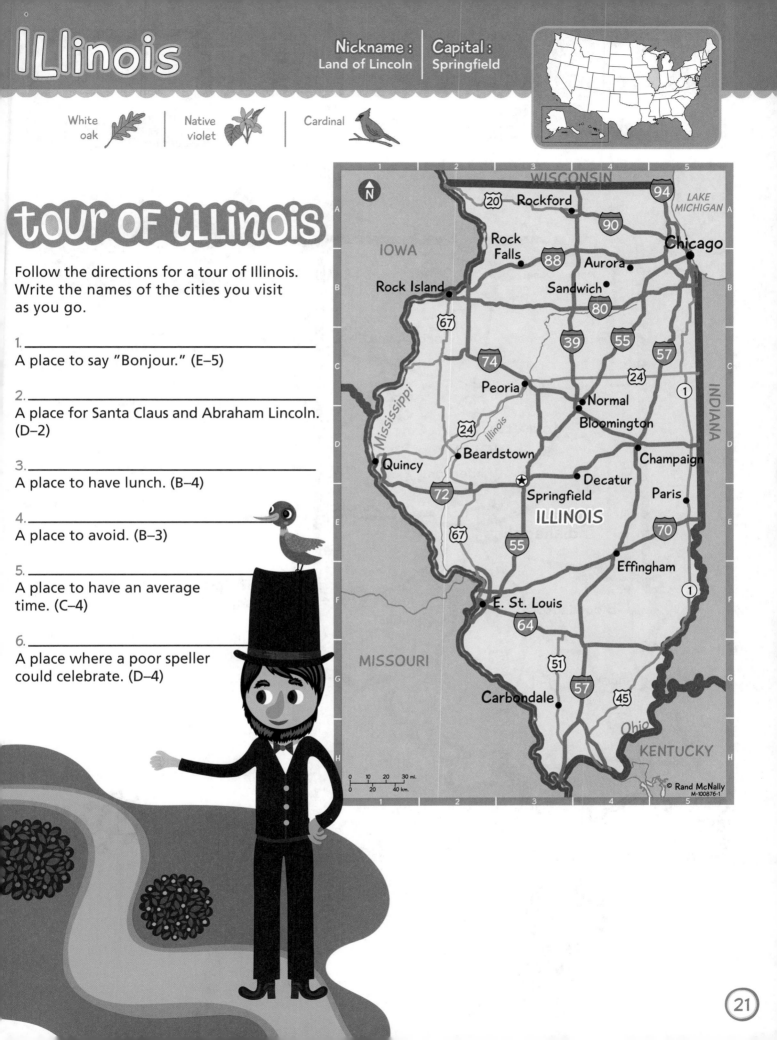

WISCONSIN
Rockford
LAKE MICHIGAN
Rock Falls
IOWA
Aurora
Chicago
Rock Island
Sandwich
Peoria
Normal
Bloomington
Quincy
Beardstown
Champaign
Decatur
Paris
Springfield
ILLINOIS
Effingham
E. St. Louis
MISSOURI
Carbondale
Ohio
KENTUCKY
INDIANA
Mississippi
Illinois

0   10   20   30 mi.
0   20   40 km.

© Rand McNally
M-100876-1

INdiana

Nickname: The Hoosier State | Capital: Indianapolis

Tulip tree | Peony | Cardinal

A DAY at THE RACES

In the Indy 500 car race it can be hard to tell who is winning. Some cars can be laps ahead of the others. Use the clues below to figure out which car is winning and which cars are coming in 2nd and 3rd.

1. None of the odd numbered cars finished in the top three.

2. The gray car didn't finish in the top three.

3. The yellow car didn't win.

4. The brown car didn't finish in the top three.

5. The red car came in right behind the orange car.

1st_____

2nd_____

3rd_____

IowA

Nickname: The Hawkeye State | Capital: Des Moines

Oak | Wild rose | Eastern goldfinch

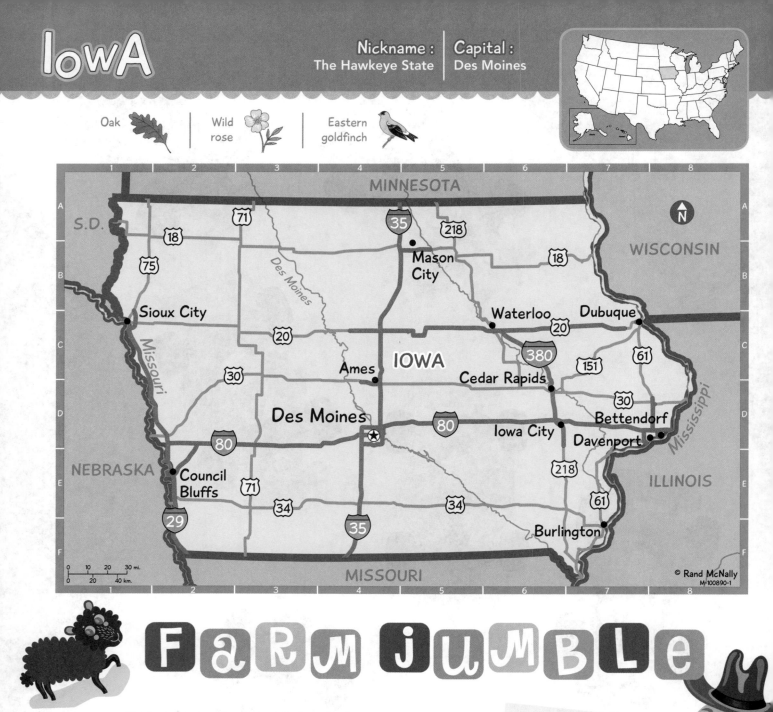

FaRm JumBLe

The names of 7 farm animals are mixed up below. Unscramble them and write the correct names in the boxes. The shaded letters, reading from top to bottom, will spell out the name of something that is made in Iowa. More of this product is made in Sioux City than in any other place in the world!

1. GIP
2. TROOSER
3. HEEPS
4. CWO
5. TOGA
6. RHOSE
7. NECKHIC

1.
2.
3.
4.
5.
6.
7.

24

KanSas

Cottonwood | Native sunflower | Western meadowlark

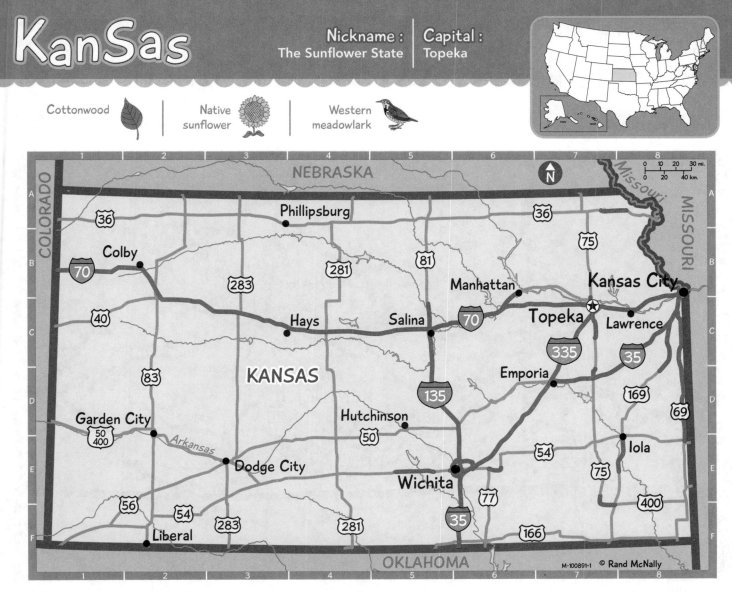

Dodge City, Kansas, was a famous town in the Old West. Circle what doesn't belong in this Old West scene.

Kentucky

Nickname: The Bluegrass State | Capital: Frankfort

Tulip poplar | Goldenrod | Cardinal

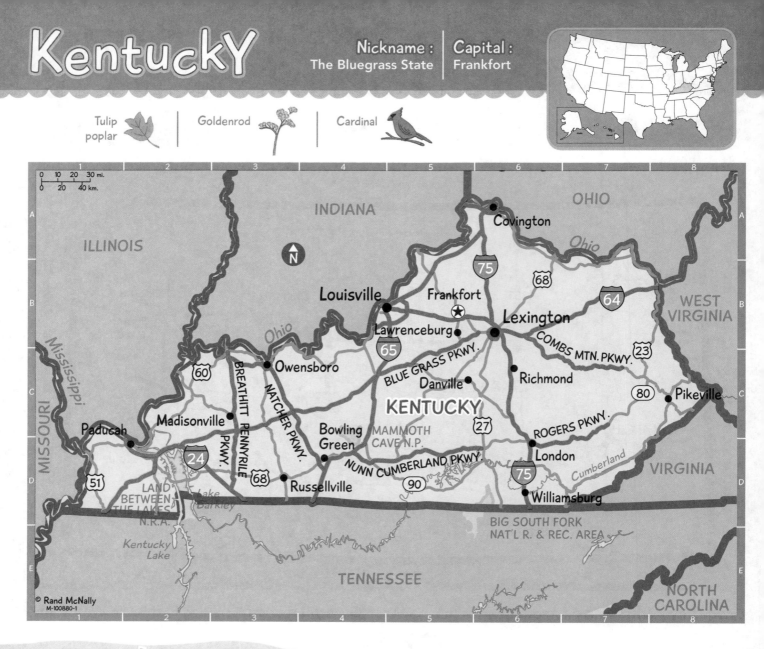

BOY Oh BOY!

The name "Ken" can be found in the first three letters of Kentucky. How many boys' names can you find hidden in the cities on the map of Kentucky?

Hint: All of the names do not occur at the beginning of the city names.

LouisiAna

Bald cypress | Magnolia | Eastern brown pelican

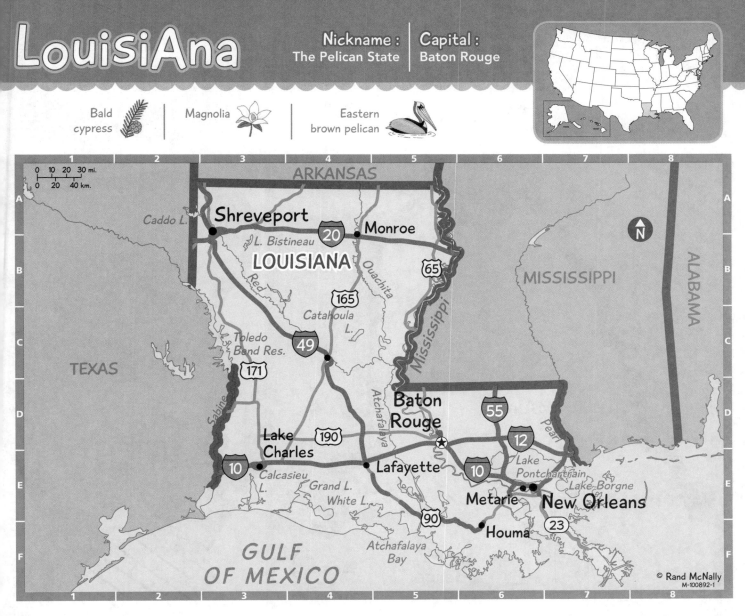

BiG RiveRs

Can you fit the names of these Louisiana rivers, bayous, and lakes into the grid? One of the lake names is in the puzzle to get you started. Hint: Counting the number of letters in the words and using the color code will help.

RIVERS: Mississippi, Red, Ouachita, Sabine, Pearl, Atchafalaya, Black

BAYOUS: Teche, Lafourche, Macon, Boeuf, Dorcheat, D'Arbonne

LAKES: Pontchartrain, Calcasieu, White, Borgne, Caddo, Bistineau, Toledo Bend Reservoir, Grand, Catahoula

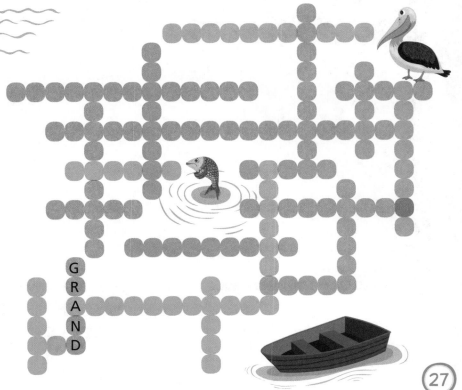

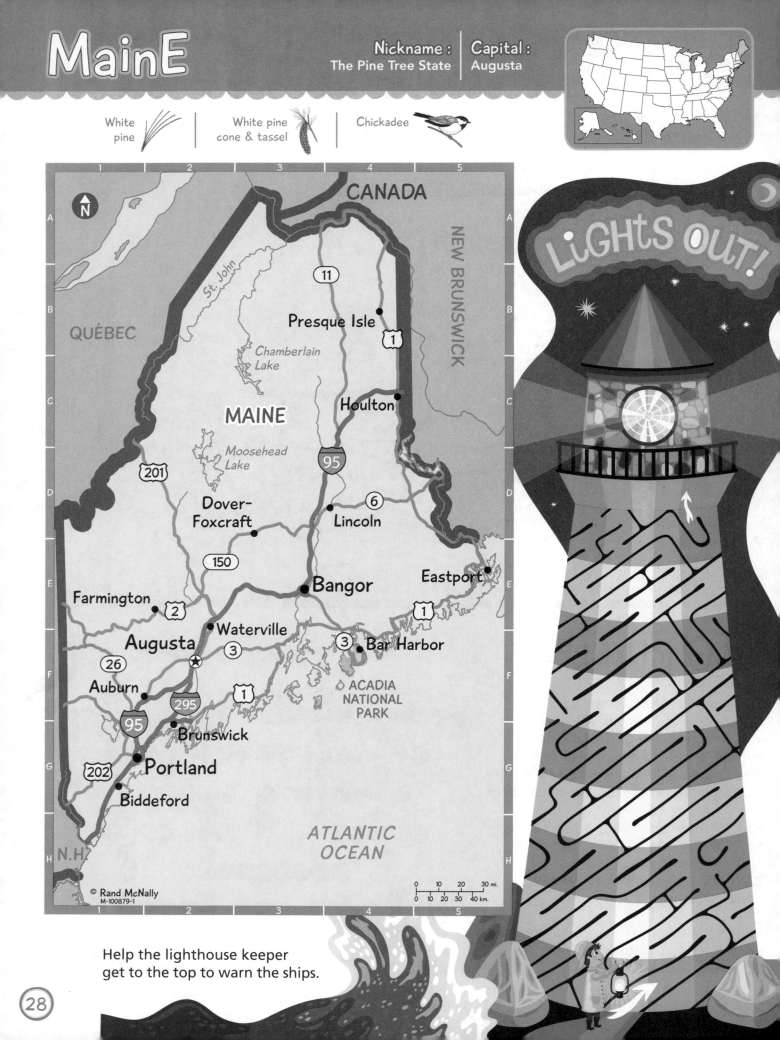

MainE

White pine

White pine cone & tassel

Chickadee

CANADA

NEW BRUNSWICK

QUÉBEC

St. John

11

Presque Isle

1

Chamberlain Lake

MAINE

Houlton

Moosehead Lake

95

201

6

Dover-Foxcraft

Lincoln

150

Eastport

Farmington

2

Bangor

Augusta

Waterville

3

1

3

Bar Harbor

26

Auburn

295

1

ACADIA NATIONAL PARK

95

Brunswick

202

Portland

Biddeford

ATLANTIC OCEAN

N.H.

© Rand McNally
M-100879-1

0 10 20 30 mi.
0 10 20 30 40 km.

LiGHtS OUT!

Help the lighthouse keeper get to the top to warn the ships.

28

MaryLanD

White oak | Black-eyed susan | Baltimore oriole

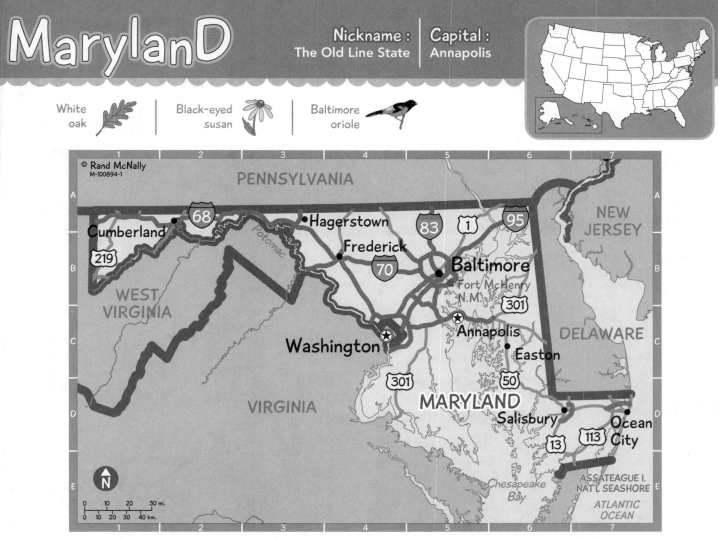

1. Oh! Say can you see, by the dawn's early light,
2. what so proudly we hailed at the twilight's last gleaming?
3. Whose broad stripes and bright stars through the perilous fight,
4. o'er the ramparts we watched were so gallantly streaming?
5. And the rockets' red glare,
6. the bombs bursting in air
7. gave proof through the night
8. that our flag was still there.
9. Oh! Say does that star-spangled banner yet wave
10. o'er the land of the free and the home of the brave?

Use the example at the right to understand the code. The letter G is in line number 1, word number 10, and letter number 3.

G
line 1
word 10
letter 3

Francis Scott Key wrote the National Anthem in Maryland during the Battle of Baltimore in the War of 1812. Solve the code to find out where he was when he wrote these famous words.

9	7	8	2	3	5	2	4	4	2	4	7	5	5
1	4	4	1	6	1	3	3	9	8	1	5	5	4
2	3	1	3	1	1	1	1	7	9	1	1	5	1

10	10	8	6	1	3	4	6	9	7	2	3	4	7
9	3	3	2	9	3	3	4	2	3	2	10	9	2
2	3	3	1	3	4	7	1	1	2	1	4	7	1

MAssachusetts

Nickname: The Bay State | **Capital:** Boston

American elm | Mayflower | Black-capped chickadee

Bay Staters

Many famous people were born in or lived in Massachusetts. The names of fifteen of them are hidden in the word search on the next page. (Only the last names are hidden.)

(JOHN) ADAMS
(LOUISA MAY) ALCOTT
(SUSAN B.) ANTHONY
(CLARA) BARTON
(EMILY) DICKINSON

(W.E.B.) DUBOIS
(RALPH WALDO) EMERSON
(BENJAMIN) FRANKLIN
(JOHN) HANCOCK
(OLIVER WENDELL) HOLMES

(WINSLOW) HOMER
(JOHN F.) KENNEDY
(EDGAR ALLAN) POE
(PAUL) REVERE
(NORMAN) ROCKWELL

```
A D R L P O E
E X I H O L M E S
F A N C D E C E R E
G R R K A H M K R A
M B A I R E E E W H
L S L N R E V H A E N
K E I S K E M N N O L A
N E O O R L C O T R L L
N N N B O I R H C Y
D N C U A N O A
V K E B D T N I D
T H O D T R Y E A
A D A M S Y U
```

MIchigan

Nickname : The Wolverine State | Capital : Lansing

White pine | Apple blossom | Robin

You are the inspector for this line of new cars in Detroit, the "Motor City." Circle the six differences between the standard and the other cars.

Standard

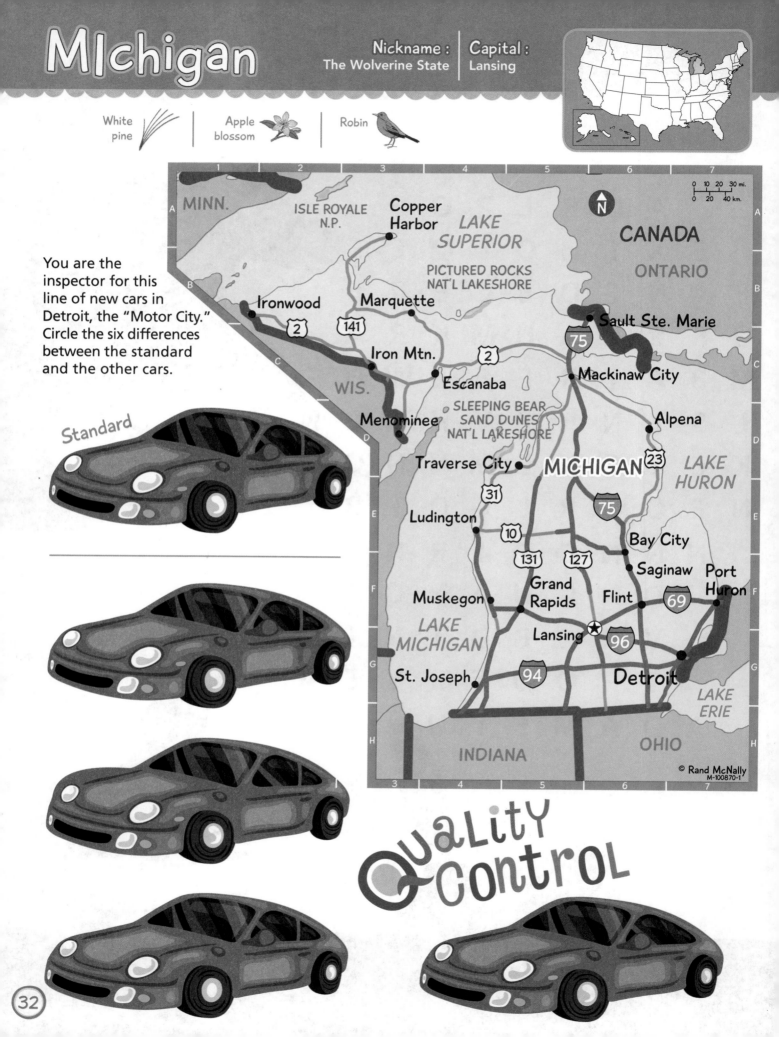

Map of Michigan

MINN.

ISLE ROYALE N.P.

Copper Harbor

LAKE SUPERIOR

CANADA

ONTARIO

PICTURED ROCKS NAT'L LAKESHORE

Ironwood 2

Marquette

141

Sault Ste. Marie 75

Iron Mtn. 2

Escanaba

Mackinaw City

WIS.

SLEEPING BEAR SAND DUNES NAT'L LAKESHORE

Alpena

Menominee

Traverse City

MICHIGAN 23

LAKE HURON

31

Ludington

75

10

Bay City

131 127

Saginaw

Port Huron

Grand Rapids

Flint

69

Muskegon

LAKE MICHIGAN

Lansing 96

St. Joseph

94

Detroit

LAKE ERIE

INDIANA

OHIO

© Rand McNally
M-100870-1

Quality Control

MiNnesota

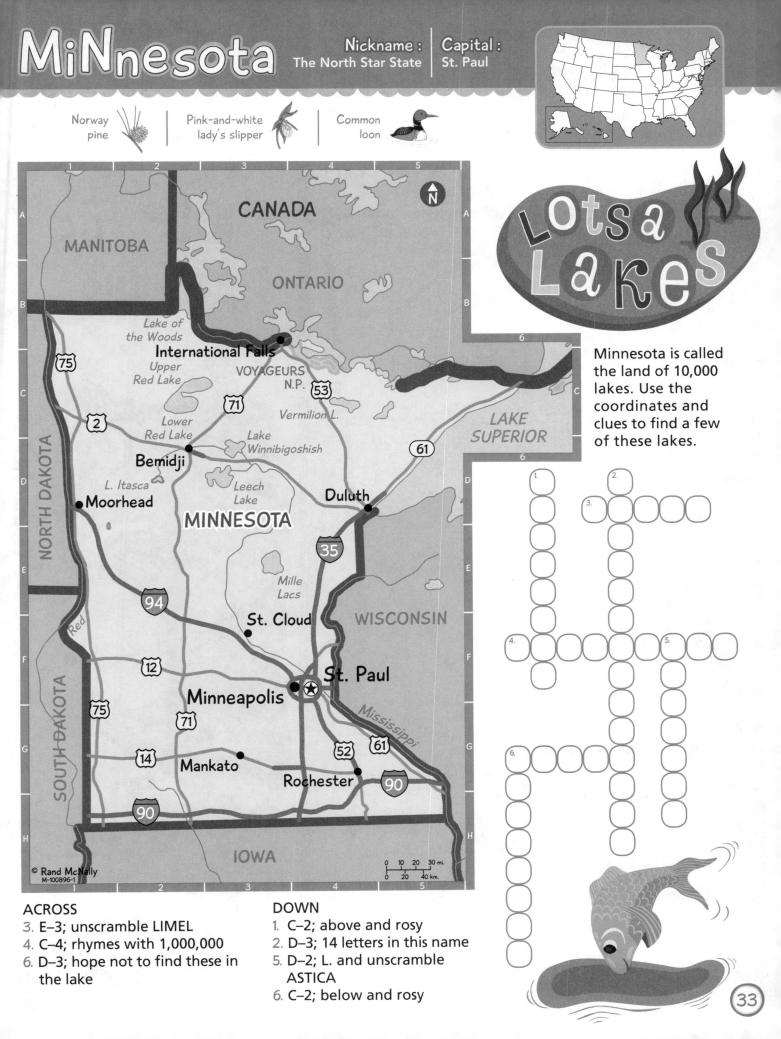

Nickname: The North Star State | Capital: St. Paul

Norway pine | Pink-and-white lady's slipper | Common loon

Lotsa Lakes

Minnesota is called the land of 10,000 lakes. Use the coordinates and clues to find a few of these lakes.

ACROSS
3. E–3; unscramble LIMEL
4. C–4; rhymes with 1,000,000
6. D–3; hope not to find these in the lake

DOWN
1. C–2; above and rosy
2. D–3; 14 letters in this name
5. D–2; L. and unscramble ASTICA
6. C–2; below and rosy

33

Nickname: The Magnolia State

Capital: Jackson

Magnolia | Magnolia | Mockingbird

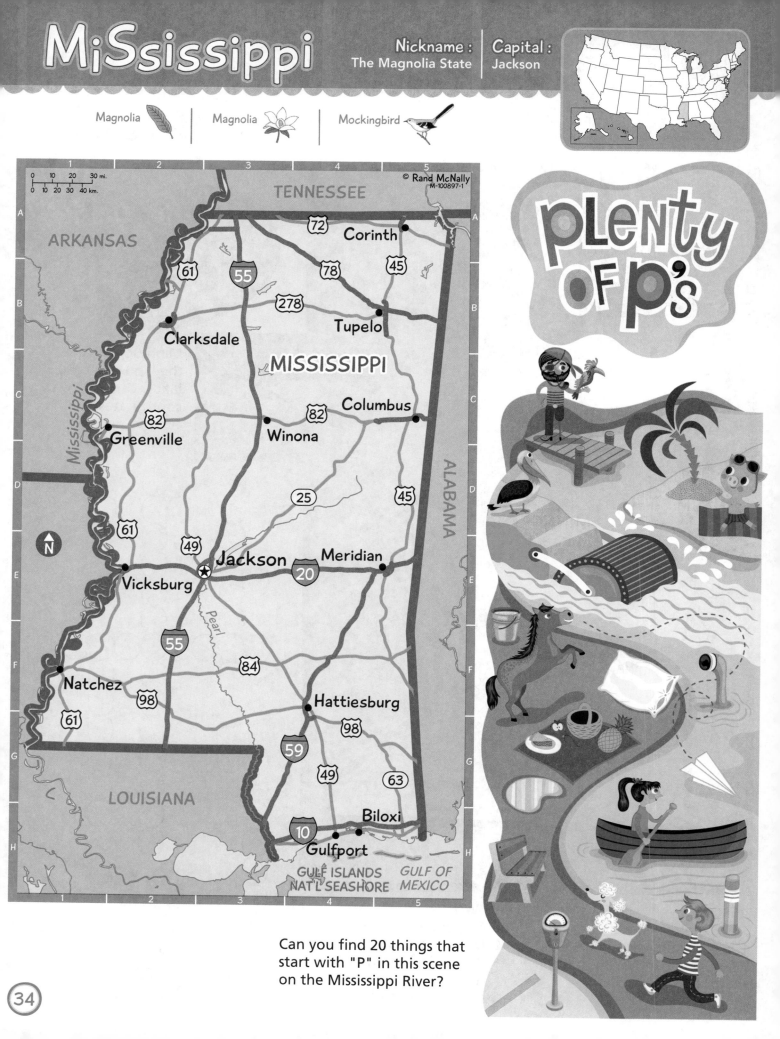

TENNESSEE

ARKANSAS

© Rand McNally
M-100897-1

Corinth

Clarksdale

Tupelo

MISSISSIPPI

Columbus

Greenville

Winona

Natchez

Vicksburg

Jackson

Meridian

ALABAMA

Hattiesburg

LOUISIANA

Biloxi

Gulfport

GULF ISLANDS NAT'L SEASHORE

GULF OF MEXICO

Mississippi

Pearl

pLeNty oF P's

Can you find 20 things that start with "P" in this scene on the Mississippi River?

MissOuri

Nickname: The Show Me State | Capital: Jefferson City

Flowering dogwood | Hawthorn blossom | Bluebird

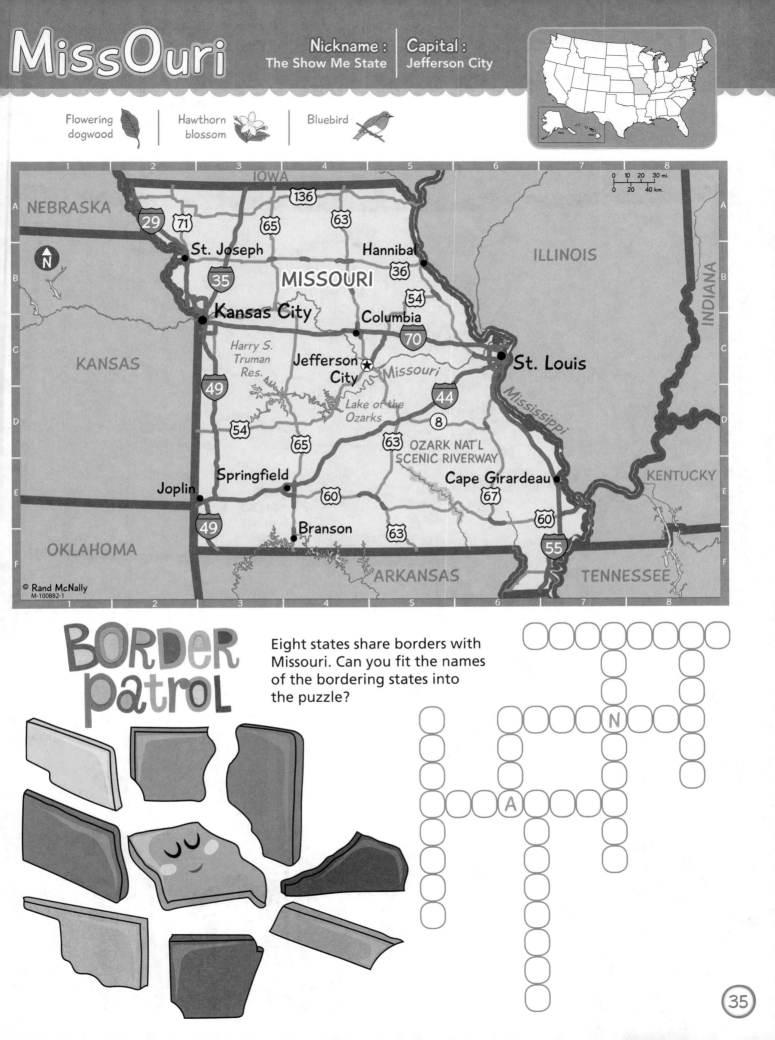

Map

- NEBRASKA
- IOWA
- 136
- 29 | 71
- 65
- 63
- St. Joseph
- Hannibal
- 35
- MISSOURI
- 36
- ILLINOIS
- INDIANA
- Kansas City
- 54
- Columbia
- 70
- St. Louis
- KANSAS
- Harry S. Truman Res.
- Jefferson City
- Missouri
- 49
- Lake of the Ozarks
- 44
- 8
- Mississippi
- 54
- 65
- 63
- OZARK NAT'L SCENIC RIVERWAY
- Springfield
- Cape Girardeau
- KENTUCKY
- Joplin
- 60
- 67
- 60
- 49
- Branson
- 63
- 55
- OKLAHOMA
- ARKANSAS
- TENNESSEE
- © Rand McNally
- M-100882-1

BORDER patrol

Eight states share borders with Missouri. Can you fit the names of the bordering states into the puzzle?

(N)
(A)

MonTana

Nickname: The Treasure State | Capital: Helena

Ponderosa pine | Bitterroot | Western meadowlark

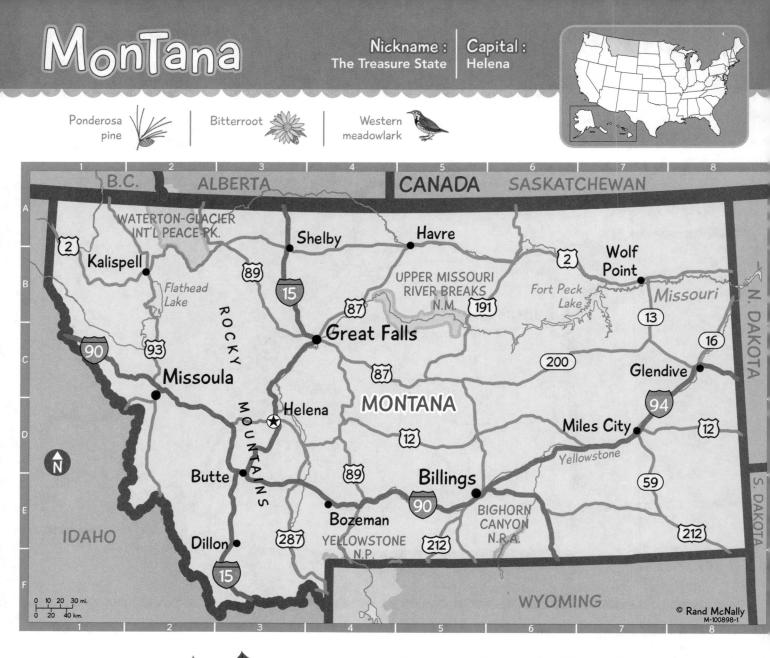

After a morning of boarding at Big Sky Resort, this snowboarder went in for lunch. When he came out, he couldn't remember where he had put his snowboard. Using the clues that he recalls, help him find his board.

SNOWBOARD SHUFFLE

1. His snowboard isn't next to a pair of skis.
2. His snowboard is not blue.
3. His snowboard is next to a blue snowboard.

NEbraska

Nickname: The Cornhusker State | Capital: Lincoln

Cottonwood | Goldenrod | Western meadowlark

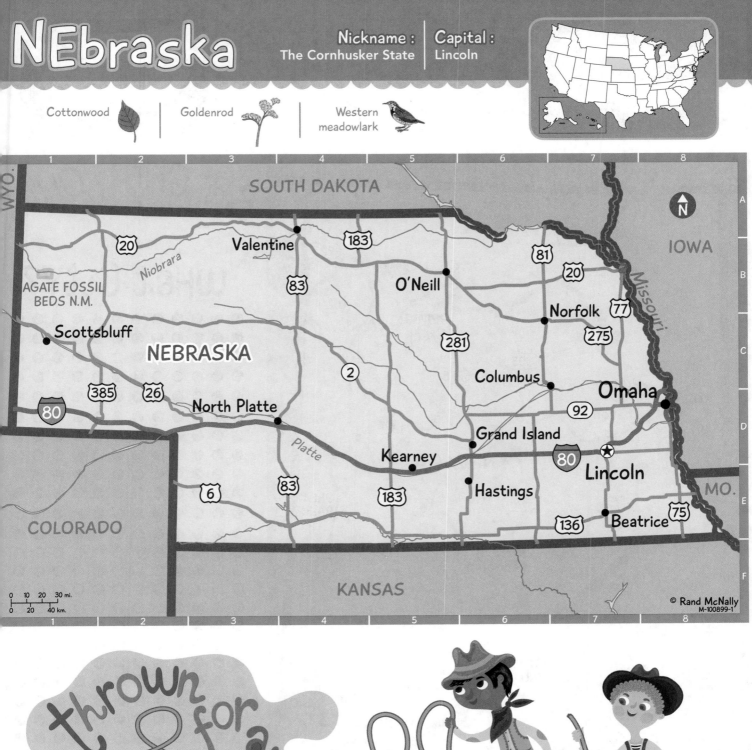

thrown for a loop

The cowboy tradition is alive and kicking in Nebraska. Here, a few cowboys have been practicing their roping tricks. Some of the ropes lying on the ground will form knots when both ends are pulled. Can you tell which ones?

NeVada

Nickname: **The Silver State** | Capital: **Carson City**

Single-leaf piñon | Sagebrush | Mountain bluebird

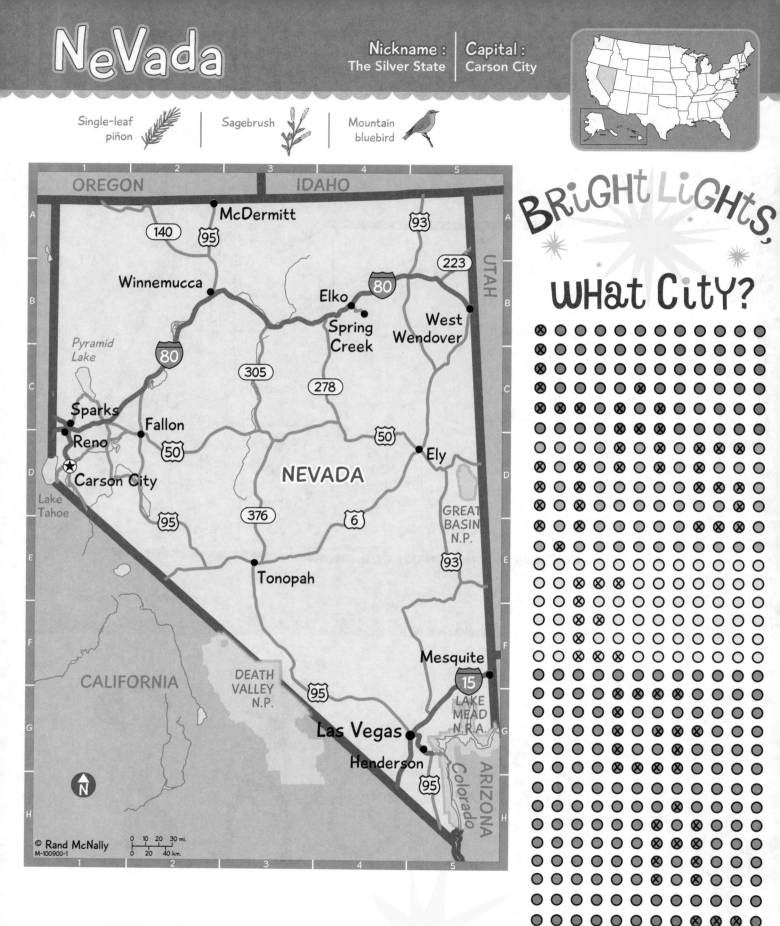

OREGON | **IDAHO**

McDermitt
140 · 95 · 93
223
Winnemucca
80
Elko
West Wendover
Spring Creek
UTAH
Pyramid Lake
80
305
278
Sparks
Fallon
50
Reno
Carson City
50
Ely
NEVADA
Lake Tahoe
95
376
6
GREAT BASIN N.P.
93
Tonopah
CALIFORNIA
DEATH VALLEY N.P.
Mesquite
15
95
LAKE MEAD N.R.A.
Las Vegas
ARIZONA
Henderson
95
Colorado

© Rand McNally
M-100900-1
0 10 20 30 mi.
0 20 40 km.

BRiGHt LiGHtS, WHat CitY?

Hidden within the colorful lights is the answer to the riddle. All you have to do is fill in the bulbs marked with an "X."

Riddle: What city has the highest electric bills in America?

38

New Hampshire

Nickname: The Granite State

Capital: Concord

White birch | Purple lilac | Purple finch

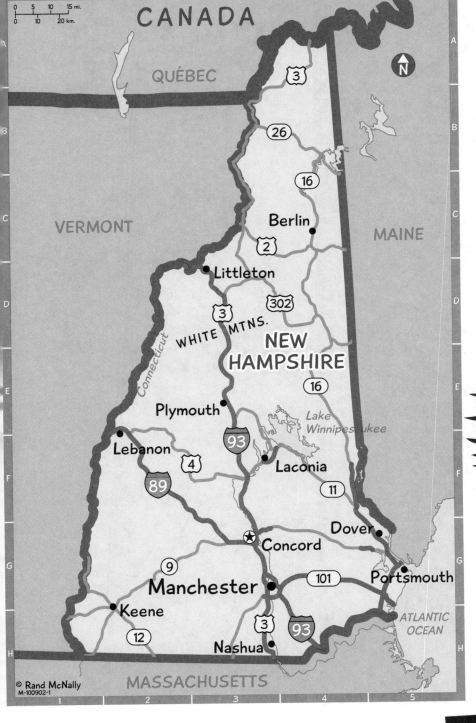

UNDER a SPeLL

How many things can you find in this scene that can only be spelled using letters found in the words NEW HAMPSHIRE?

© Rand McNally
M-100902-1

Red oak | Purple violet | Eastern goldfinch

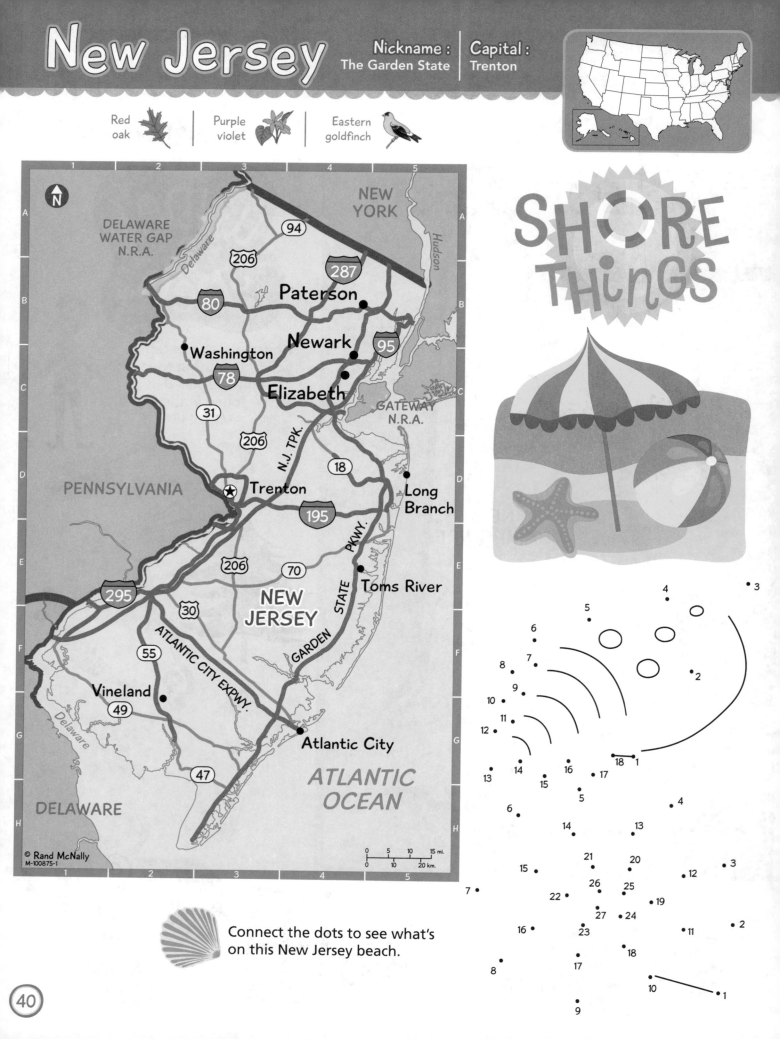

N

DELAWARE WATER GAP N.R.A.

NEW YORK

94
206
287
Paterson
80
Newark
95
Washington
78
Elizabeth
31
GATEWAY N.R.A.
206
N.J. TPK.
18
PENNSYLVANIA
Trenton
195
Long Branch
206
70
STATE PKWY.
Toms River
NEW JERSEY
295
30
GARDEN
55
ATLANTIC CITY EXPWY.
Vineland
49
Atlantic City
47
ATLANTIC OCEAN
DELAWARE
Delaware
Hudson

© Rand McNally
M-100875-1

0   5   10   15 mi.
0   10   20 km.

SH☐RE THiNGS

Connect the dots to see what's on this New Jersey beach.

New Mexico

Nickname: Land of Enchantment | **Capital:** Santa Fe

Piñon pine | Yucca | Roadrunner

© Rand McNally
M-100903-1

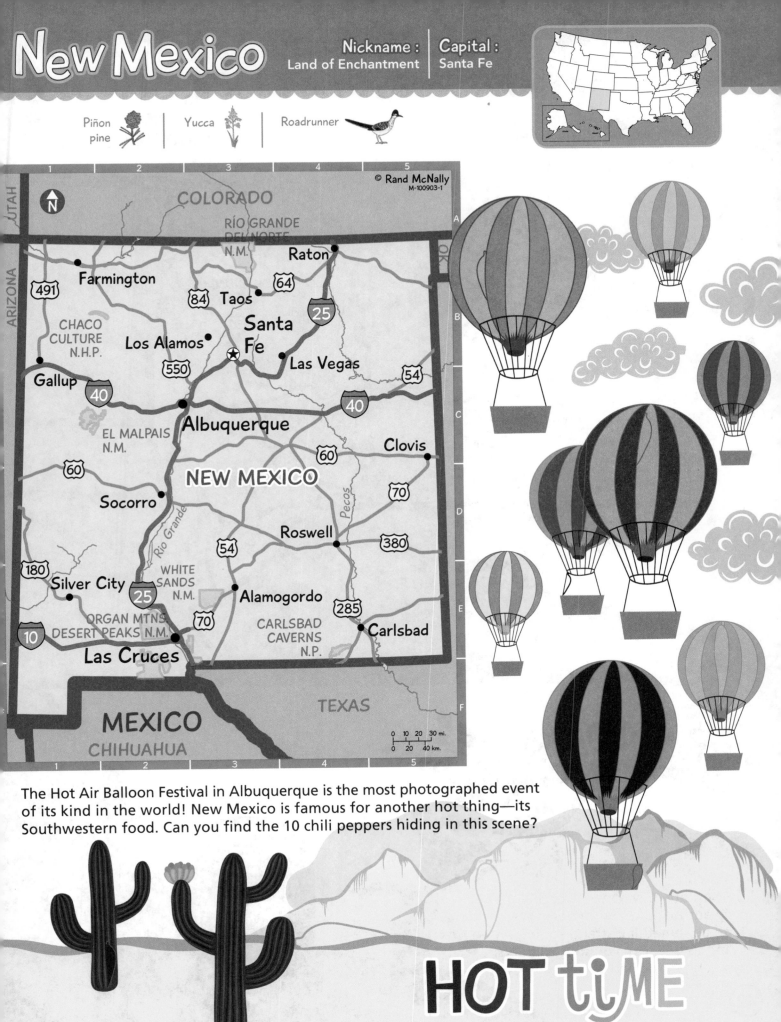

The Hot Air Balloon Festival in Albuquerque is the most photographed event of its kind in the world! New Mexico is famous for another hot thing—its Southwestern food. Can you find the 10 chili peppers hiding in this scene?

HOT tiME

New York

Nickname : The Empire State

Capital : Albany

Sugar maple | Rose | Red-breasted bluebird

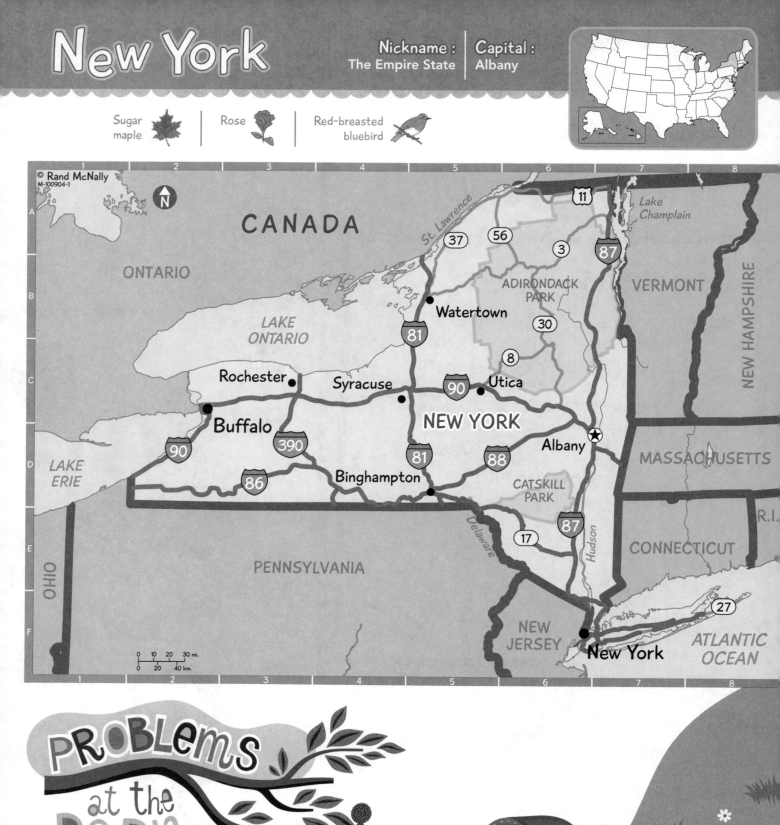

PROBLEMS at the PARK

The state of New York has many beautiful parks, but there seems to be something strange going on in this one. Can you spot 10 things wrong in the park?

North Carolina

Nickname: The Tar Heel State

Capital: Raleigh

Pine | Dogwood | Cardinal

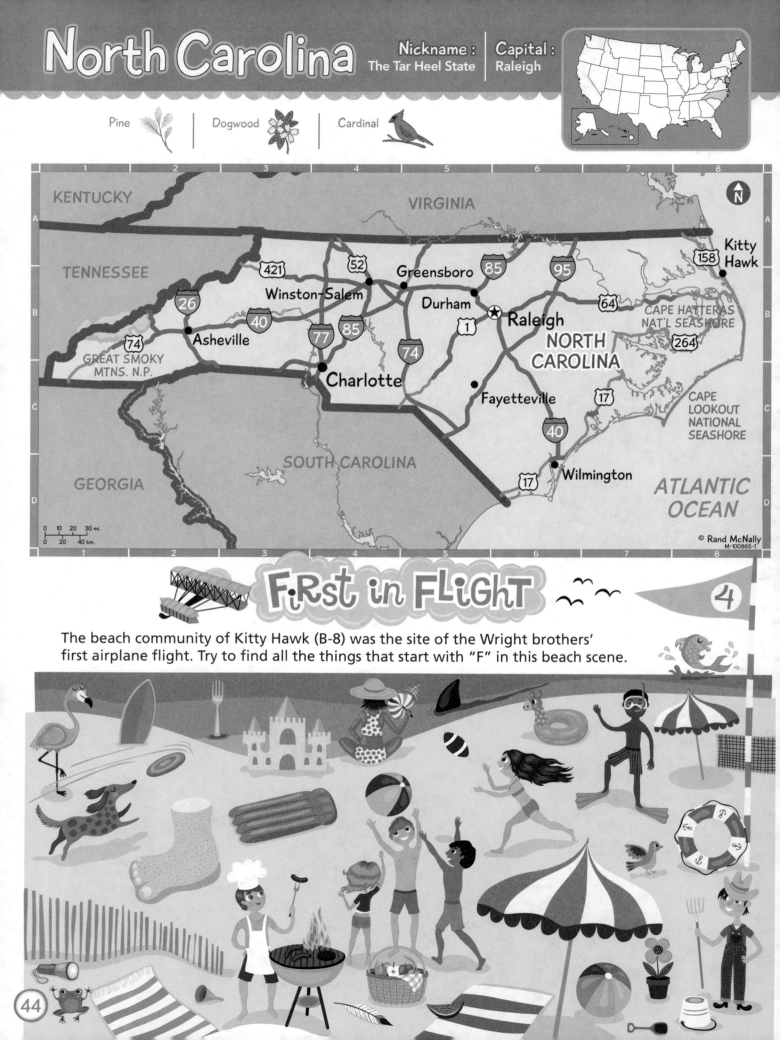

First in Flight

4

The beach community of Kitty Hawk (B-8) was the site of the Wright brothers' first airplane flight. Try to find all the things that start with "F" in this beach scene.

© Rand McNally
M-100865-1

North Dakota

Nickname: The Peace Garden State | Capital: Bismarck

American elm | Wild prairie rose | Western meadowlark

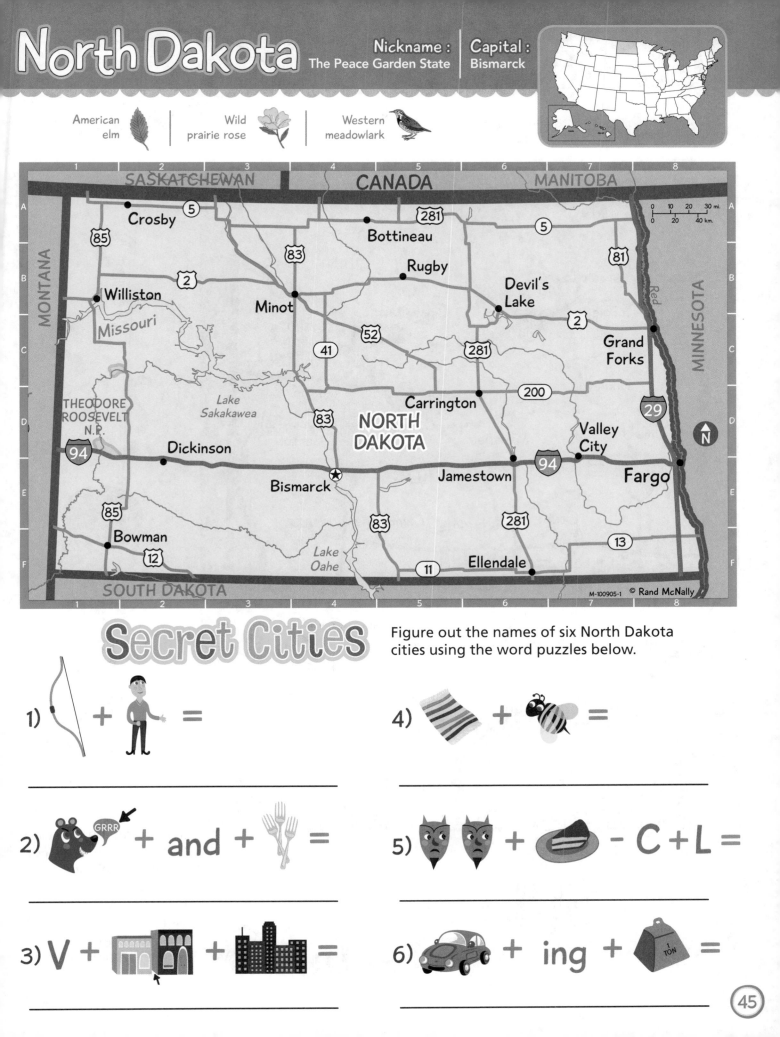

Secret Cities

Figure out the names of six North Dakota cities using the word puzzles below.

1) 🏹 + 🧍 = _____

2) 🐻 GRRR + and + 🍴 = _____

3) V + 🏛️ + 🏙️ = _____

4) 〰️ + 🐝 = _____

5) 👹👹 + 🎩 - C + L = _____

6) 🚗 + ing + ⬛ TON = _____

45

OHio

Nickname: The Buckeye State | Capital: Columbus

Buckeye | Scarlet carnation | Cardinal

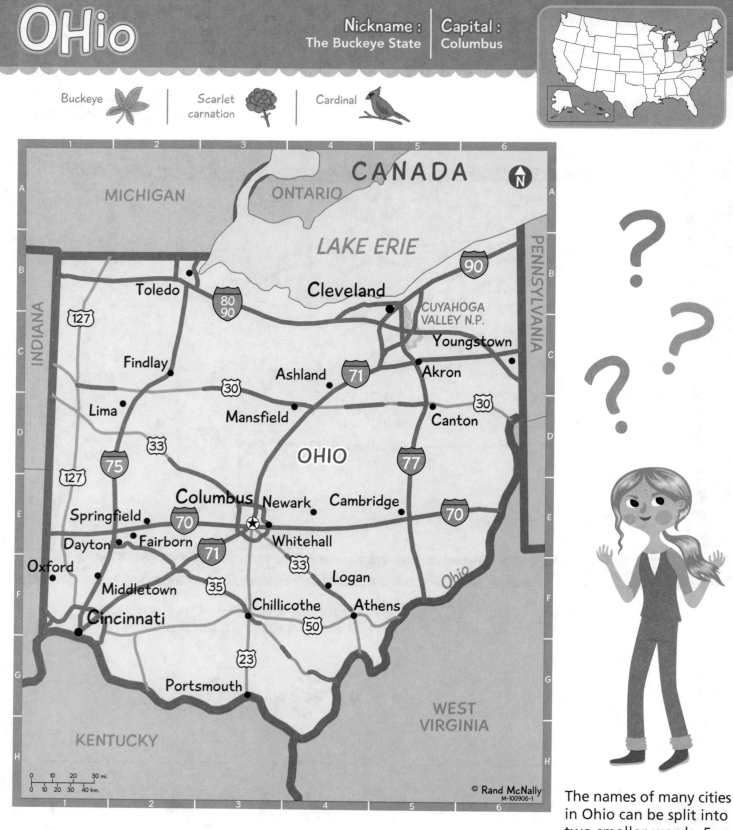

SpLit Cities

The names of many cities in Ohio can be split into two smaller words. For example, DAY and TON go together to form DAYTON. Match the words in column A with the words in column B to spell 12 Ohio cities. All of the cities are listed on the map.

Column A	Column B
FIND	LAND
NEW	MOUTH
ASH	FIELD
CAN	TOWN
WHITE	ARK
SPRING	TON
LOG	BORN
AT	AN
PORTS	FORD
OX	LAY
FAIR	HALL
MIDDLE	HENS

Redbud | Mistletoe | Scissor-tailed flycatcher

COLO. | KANSAS | MISSOURI

56 | 54 | 64
• Guymon

N

183 | Enid

60 | 81 | 35

OKLAHOMA

Clinton
Oklahoma City ★

40 | 44 | 183 | 44 | 35

62 | Lawton

TEXAS | Ardmore | Red

Bartlesville | 169 | Miami | 44
60 | Tulsa | 412 | ARK.
Stillwater | 59
177 | Muskogee | Sallisaw
Okmulgee | 40
Shawnee | INDIAN NATION
Ada | 69 | 271
3 | 259 | TPK
Idabel

0 10 20 30 mi.
0 20 40 km.

© Rand McNally
M-100869-1

Scrambled Cities

Unscramble the names of these Oklahoma towns and you'll be OK!

DINE (B-5) _____

BILEAD (E-8) _____

LOWTAN (E-5) _____

WLASSAIL (C-8) _____

LEEKOMUG (C-7) _____

MOUNGY (A-2) _____

USALT (B-7) _____

AMIMI (A-8) _____

SHEENWA (C-6) _____

TALLIWERTS (B-6) _____

ORegon

Nickname: The Beaver State | Capital: Salem

Douglas fir | Oregon grape | Western meadowlark

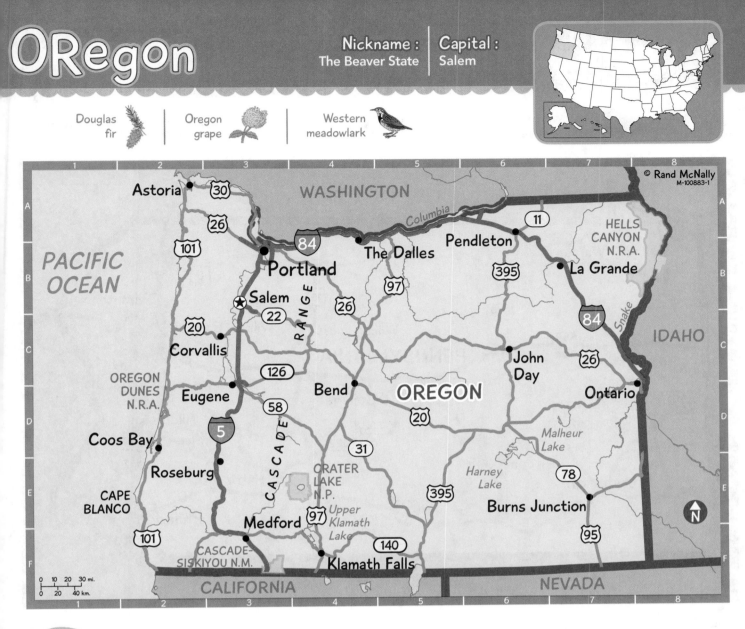

WASHINGTON

Astoria · 30
26
101
84
Portland
Salem · 22
RANGE
20
Corvallis
126
OREGON DUNES N.R.A.
Eugene
58
CASCADE
Coos Bay
5
Roseburg
CAPE BLANCO
101
Medford
97
CASCADE-SISKIYOU N.M.
Klamath Falls
140

The Dalles
97
26
Pendleton · 11
395
La Grande
84
Snake
IDAHO

John Day
26
OREGON
20
Ontario

Malheur Lake
31
Harney Lake
78
395
Burns Junction
95

Columbia

HELLS CANYON N.R.A.

Upper Klamath Lake

PACIFIC OCEAN

CALIFORNIA | NEVADA

© Rand McNally
M-100883-1

0 10 20 30 mi.
0 20 40 km.

N

Dive In

These two tide pools on the Oregon coast are almost exactly alike. Can you spot the differences between them?

PennsylvAnia

Nickname: The Keystone State
Capital: Harrisburg

Hemlock | Mountain laurel | Ruffed grouse

two of a kind

Two of the squares in this Pennsylvania Dutch quilt are exactly the same. Can you find them?

50

Rhode Island

Nickname: The Ocean State | Capital: Providence

Red maple | Violet | Rhode Island red

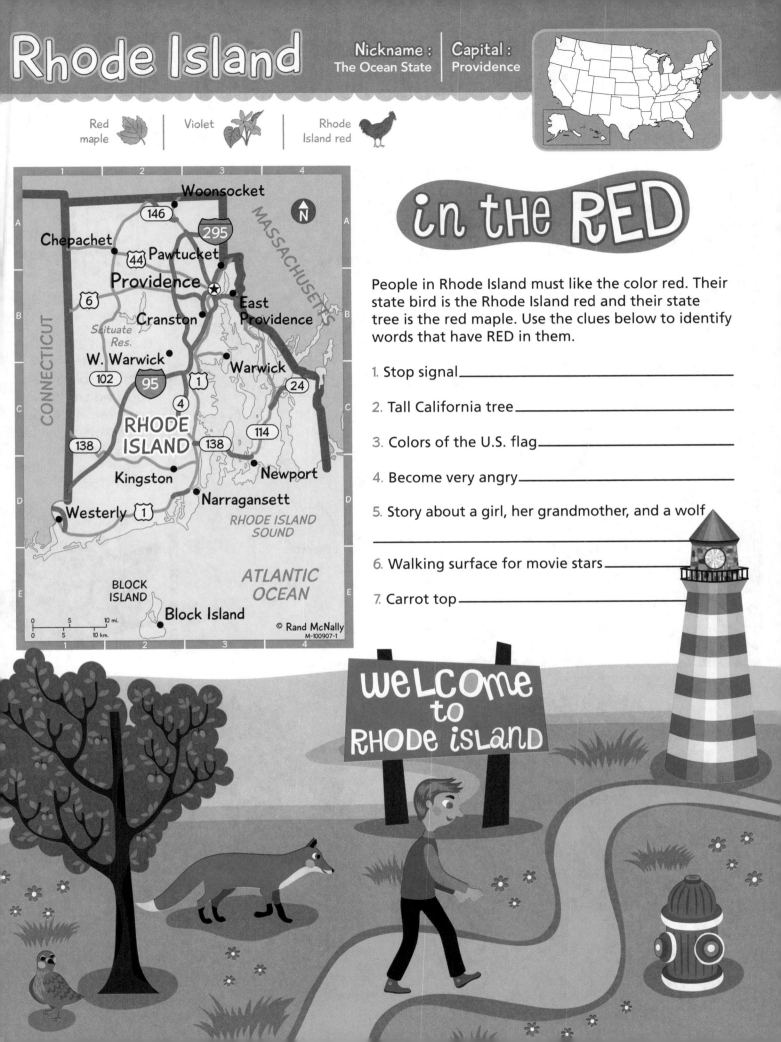

Map

Woonsocket
146
Chepachet
295
MASSACHUSETTS
44 Pawtucket
Providence
6
East Providence
Cranston
Scituate Res.
W. Warwick
102
95
1 Warwick
24
4
RHODE ISLAND
114
138
138
Kingston
Newport
Westerly 1
Narragansett
RHODE ISLAND SOUND
CONNECTICUT
BLOCK ISLAND
ATLANTIC OCEAN
Block Island

0 5 10 mi.
0 5 10 km.

© Rand McNally
M-100907-1

in THE RED

People in Rhode Island must like the color red. Their state bird is the Rhode Island red and their state tree is the red maple. Use the clues below to identify words that have RED in them.

1. Stop signal_____

2. Tall California tree_____

3. Colors of the U.S. flag_____

4. Become very angry_____

5. Story about a girl, her grandmother, and a wolf
_____

6. Walking surface for movie stars_____

7. Carrot top_____

WELCOME to RHODE iSLAND

South Carolina

Nickname: The Palmetto State | Capital: Columbia

Palmetto | Carolina jessamine | Carolina wren

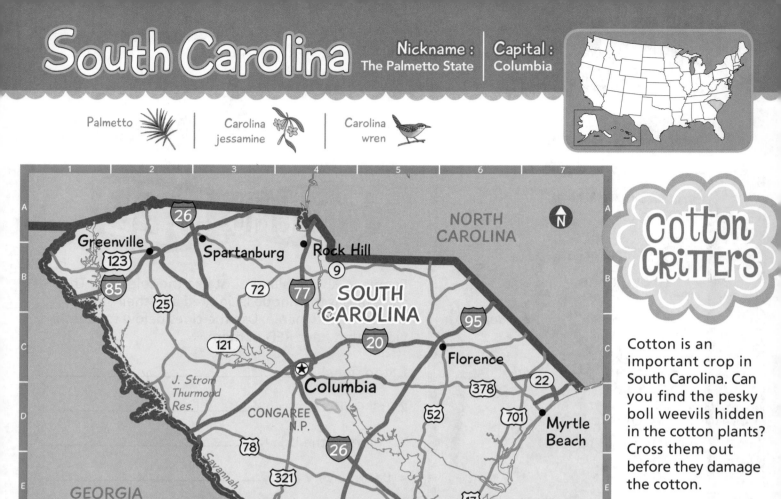

Cotton CRITTERS

Cotton is an important crop in South Carolina. Can you find the pesky boll weevils hidden in the cotton plants? Cross them out before they damage the cotton.

South Dakota

Black Hills spruce | Pasque flower | Chinese ring-necked pheasant

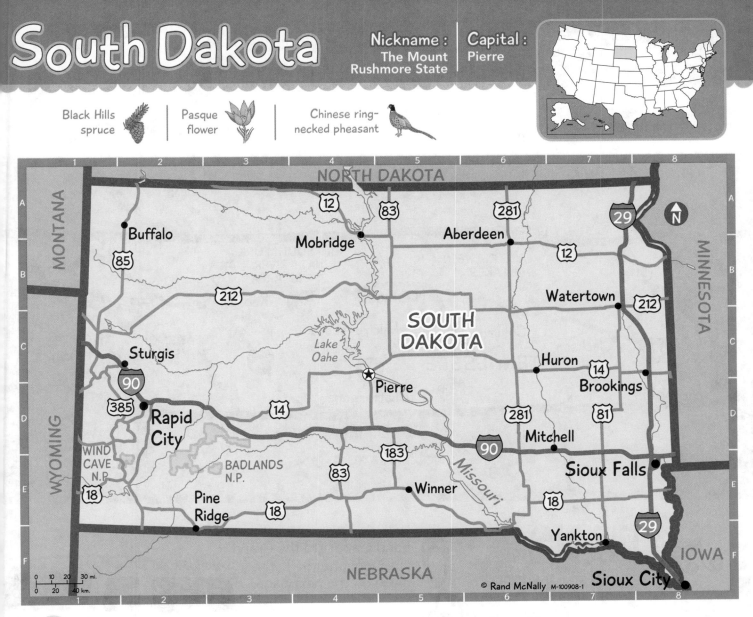

Wild & Wooly

The pictures below show the steps in making a sweater—starting with shearing a sheep for wool. However, the pictures are not in the right order. If you write the letters in the corner of the pictures in the order in which they should be placed, the letters will complete a fact about South Dakota.

TeNnessee

Nickname: The Volunteer State | **Capital:** Nashville

Tulip tree | Iris | Mockingbird

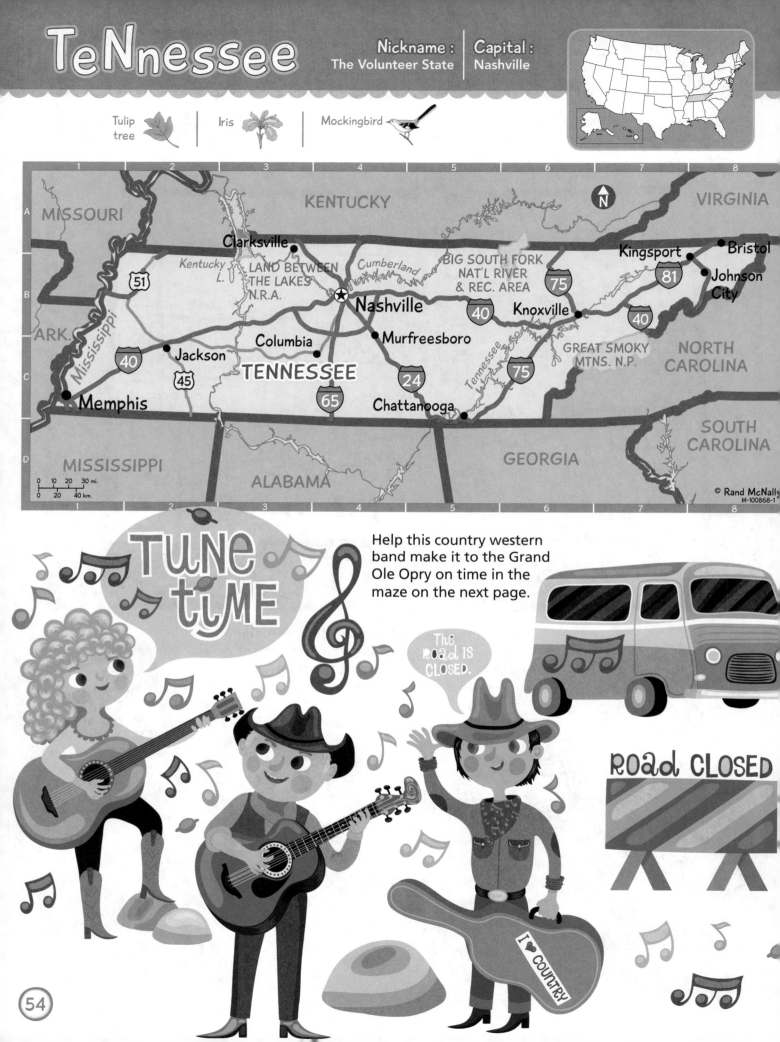

Tune Time

Help this country western band make it to the Grand Ole Opry on time in the maze on the next page.

The ROAD IS CLOSED.

ROAD CLOSED

I ♥ COUNTRY

TeXas

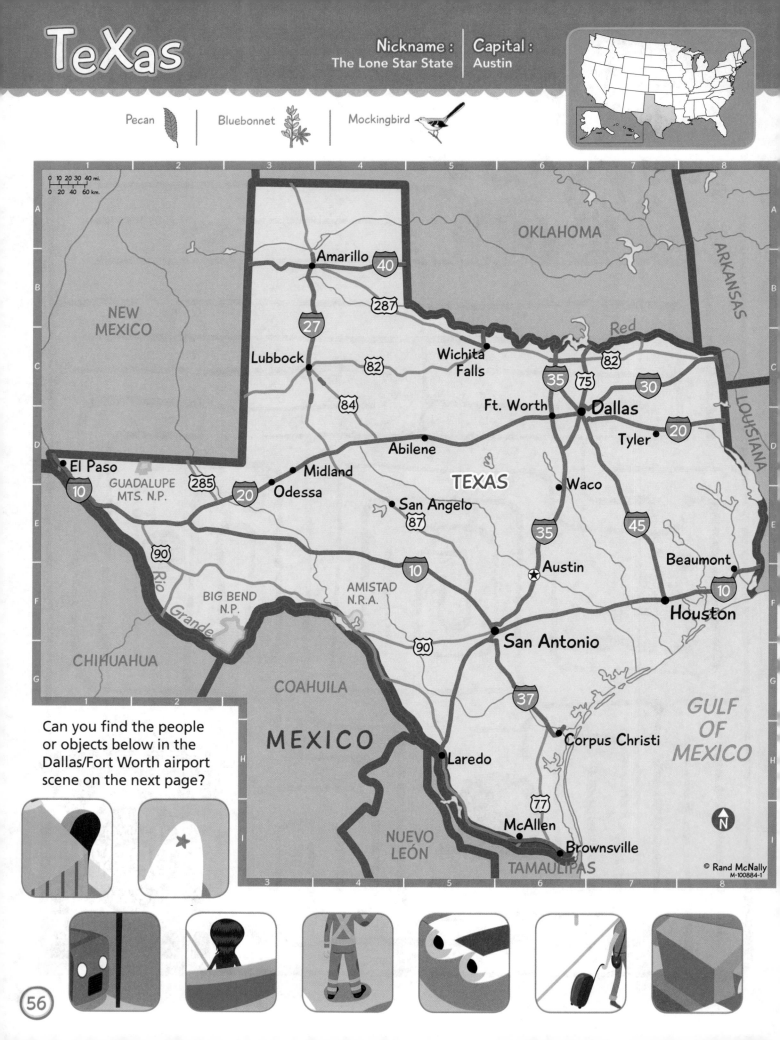

Nickname:
The Lone Star State

Capital:
Austin

Pecan | Bluebonnet | Mockingbird

0 10 20 30 40 mi.
0 20 40 60 km.

OKLAHOMA

NEW MEXICO

ARKANSAS

Amarillo 40

287

27

Red

Lubbock

82

Wichita Falls

82

35 75

30

LOUISIANA

84

Ft. Worth

Dallas

Tyler 20

Abilene

TEXAS

Waco

El Paso

10

GUADALUPE MTS. N.P.

285

Midland

20

Odessa

San Angelo

87

45

10

35

Austin

Beaumont

90

Rio Grande

BIG BEND N.P.

AMISTAD N.R.A.

10

Houston

CHIHUAHUA

90

San Antonio

COAHUILA

37

GULF OF MEXICO

Can you find the people or objects below in the Dallas/Fort Worth airport scene on the next page?

MEXICO

Corpus Christi

Laredo

N

© Rand McNally
M-100884-1

77

NUEVO LEÓN

McAllen

Brownsville

TAMAULIPAS

UTah

Blue spruce | Sego lily | American seagull

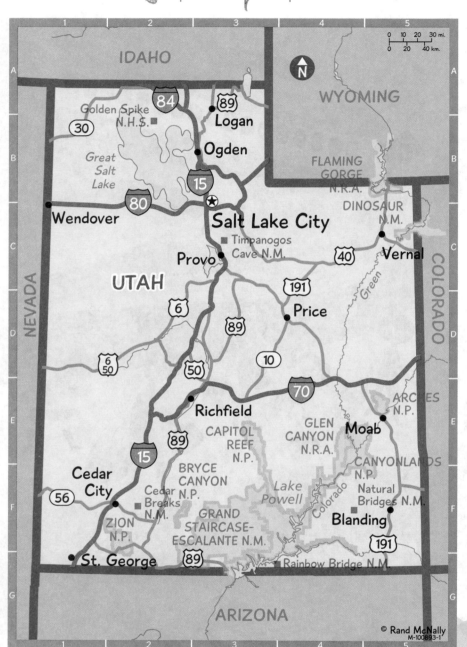

© Rand McNally
M-100893-1

Utah is home to many National Parks and Monuments. Circle the names, listed below the map, in the puzzle.

T	G	R	P	P	H	B	L	S	T	I	Y	T
T	L	I	N	E	S	A	R	C	H	E	S	C
A	E	B	A	O	R	E	Z	Q	R	O	M	H
Z	N	N	T	P	D	I	N	O	S	A	U	R
R	C	O	U	L	E	N	N	B	K	I	R	I
O	A	O	R	E	F	G	S	G	N	T	A	S
L	N	T	A	O	E	X	D	O	Z	B	D	Q
N	Y	F	L	F	G	G	I	L	L	I	B	K
G	O	G	B	E	C	W	N	D	A	W	O	E
L	N	K	R	A	P	S	H	E	C	V	Y	N
A	S	T	I	R	D	O	U	N	H	R	R	D
D	D	A	D	T	E	N	D	S	B	O	C	R
E	T	E	G	H	V	P	L	P	A	I	H	A
N	X	R	E	O	Y	T	S	I	M	I	S	I
S	O	R	S	K	B	R	A	K	N	S	O	V
C	A	P	I	T	O	L	R	E	E	F	G	S
M	G	I	L	K	B	I	I	J	R	I	O	O
A	Q	R	L	E	B	S	H	O	A	O	N	G
O	J	C	R	A	Y	A	D	C	L	N	A	H
C	A	N	Y	O	N	L	A	N	D	S	P	C
T	A	H	H	R	N	I	M	L	A	W	M	I
R	C	A	L	E	X	S	Y	T	L	P	I	N
S	K	A	E	R	B	R	A	D	E	C	T	C

ARCHES

CANYONLANDS

CAPITOL REEF

CEDAR BREAKS

DINOSAUR

GLEN CANYON

GOLDEN SPIKE

NATURAL BRIDGES

TIMPANOGOS

ZION

PARK PLACE

VeRMONT

Sugar maple | Red clover | Hermit thrush

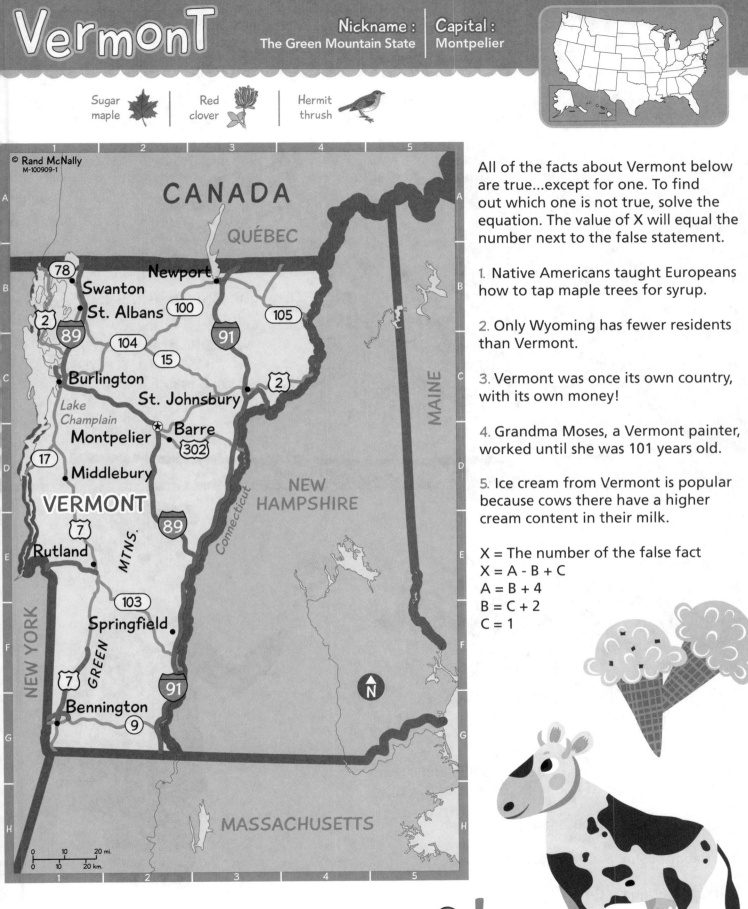

© Rand McNally
M-100909-1

All of the facts about Vermont below are true...except for one. To find out which one is not true, solve the equation. The value of X will equal the number next to the false statement.

1. Native Americans taught Europeans how to tap maple trees for syrup.

2. Only Wyoming has fewer residents than Vermont.

3. Vermont was once its own country, with its own money!

4. Grandma Moses, a Vermont painter, worked until she was 101 years old.

5. Ice cream from Vermont is popular because cows there have a higher cream content in their milk.

X = The number of the false fact
$X = A - B + C$
$A = B + 4$
$B = C + 2$
$C = 1$

UNBELiEVABLE!

VirginiA

Nickname: Old Dominion | Capital: Richmond

Dogwood | Dogwood | Cardinal

COLONiaL CLUes

This Virginia city was the center of politics and culture in colonial times. Use the clues to find out the name of this city.

1. It's about 50 miles southeast of Richmond.

2. It's about 35 miles northwest of Norfolk.

3. It's at coordinate C-7.

The city is _____

WAshington

Western hemlock | Coast rhododendron | Willow goldfinch

In the spaces provided, write the **last** letters of the objects shown in the boxes. When you're finished, the letters will spell out the name of an event that was started in 1909 by Sonora Louise Smart Dodd in Spokane, Washington.

__ __ __ __ __ __ , __

__ __ __

West Virginia

Sugar maple | Rhododendron | Cardinal

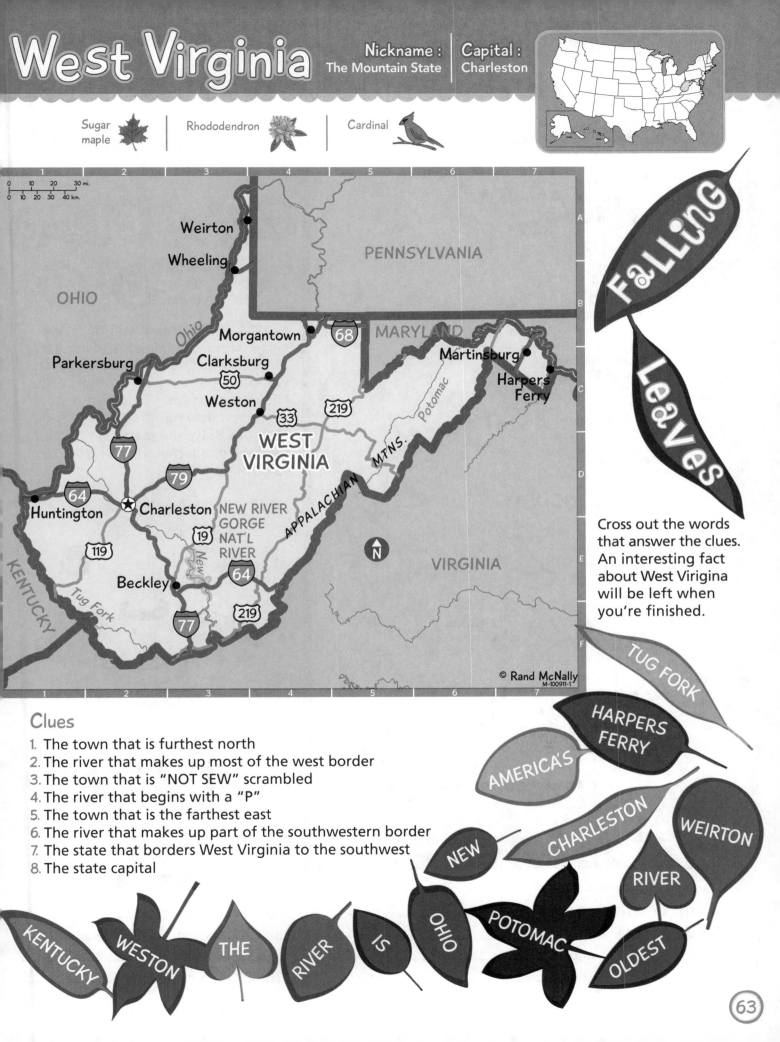

FALLING LEAVES

Cross out the words that answer the clues. An interesting fact about West Viriginia will be left when you're finished.

Clues

1. The town that is furthest north
2. The river that makes up most of the west border
3. The town that is "NOT SEW" scrambled
4. The river that begins with a "P"
5. The town that is the farthest east
6. The river that makes up part of the southwestern border
7. The state that borders West Virginia to the southwest
8. The state capital

TUG FORK
HARPERS FERRY
AMERICA'S
NEW
CHARLESTON
WEIRTON
RIVER
KENTUCKY
WESTON
THE
RIVER
IS
OHIO
POTOMAC
OLDEST

WIsconsin

Nickname: The Badger State | Capital: Madison

Sugar maple | Wood violet | Robin

CLOWNING AROUND

In 1884, five brothers held their first circus with farm animals and jugglers in Wisconsin. Over time, it became the world-famous Ringling Brothers Circus. Find out what town held that first event and now has the Circus World Museum. Solve the puzzle below and read the one-letter answers from top to bottom.

1. A letter in BEAR, but not in TRAPEZE. _____
2. A letter in LAKE and MICHIGAN. _____
3. A letter in SPARTA and MERRILL. _____
4. A letter in SUGAR and MAPLE. _____
5. A letter in BRIE, but not in AMERICAN. _____
6. A letter in HOLSTEIN and COW. _____
7. A letter in TRACTOR, but not in CART. _____

WYoming

Cottonwood | Rhododendron | Western meadowlark

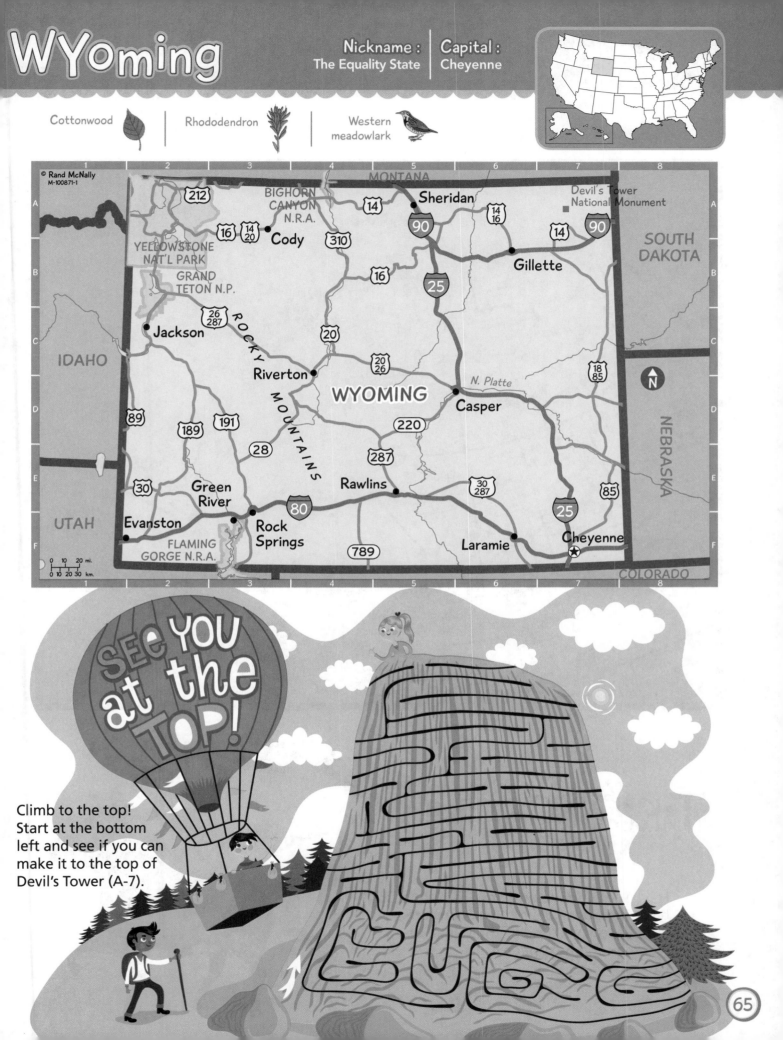

Climb to the top! Start at the bottom left and see if you can make it to the top of Devil's Tower (A-7).

SEE YOU at the TOP!

65

Canada

Capital: Ottawa

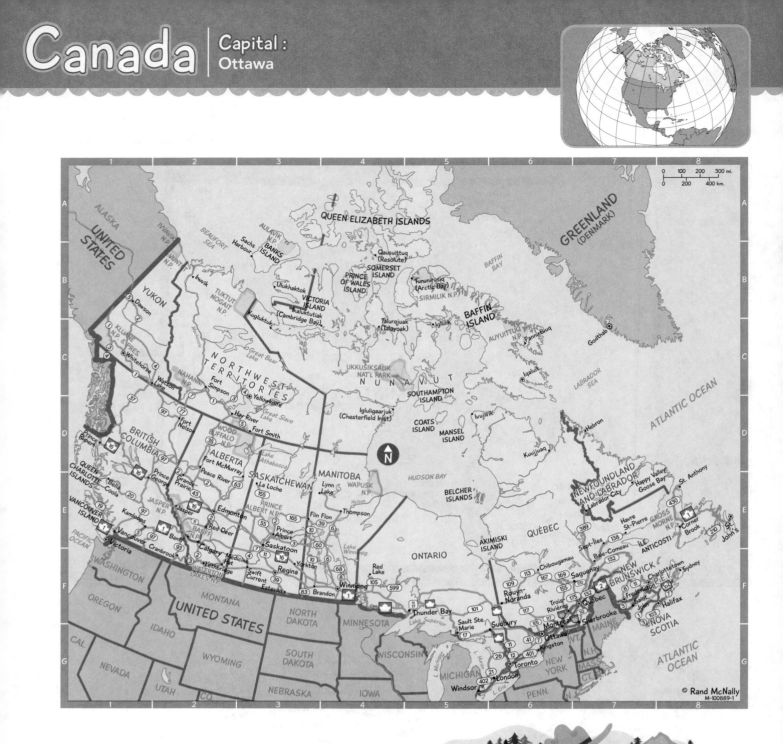

Take a Gander!

Hey! That Canadaian goose shouldn't be flying upside down! How many other mistakes can you find in the Canadian scene on the next page?

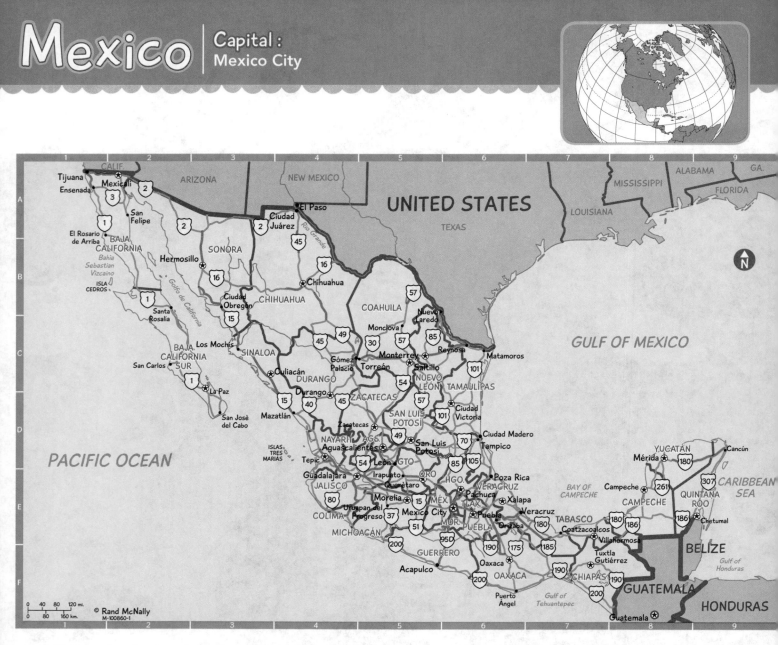

1. This body of water is to the east of Quintana Roo.

2. This city is in the northwest corner of the country.

3. This state on the south of the Bay of Campeche has the same name as a spicy sauce.

4. This food is a flat bread made from corn.

5. This river, or *rio*, forms much of the border between Mexico and the U.S.

6. This cliff-diving location is the southernmost point on highway 95D.

7. This city's name is a combination of Mexico and California.

8. This state in northern Mexico shares its name with a breed of dogs.

9. This body of water lies west of the Baja Peninsula.

10. This country lies east of Chiapas.

11. As you take highway 45 north, the last city you go through before leaving Mexico is _____.

12. This city is directly across the border to the north of question #11.

13. This country is south of Quintana Roo.

14. This "little beautiful" city is the capital city of the state of Sonora.

SOUTH OF the BORDER

Cross out the words in the puzzle that answer the questions on the opposite page. An interesting fact about Mexico will be left when you're finished. Read it from top to bottom.

MEXICANS

TIJUANA
BELIZE
WERO
ACAPULCO
EL PASO
KNOWN
CIUDAD JUAREZ
the
men
MEXICALI
of

RIO GRANDE

ONCE

CARIBBEAN SEA

GUATEMALA

TORTILLA

AS

CHIHUAHUA

HERMOSILLO

CORN

PACIFIC OCEAN

TABASCO

License Plate Game

Keep an eye out for license plates from all over the United States. Cross off the state when you see its plate.

Alabama	Hawaii	Massachusetts	New Mexico	South Dakota
Alaska	Idaho	Michigan	New York	Tennessee
Arizona	Illinois	Minnesota	North Carolina	Texas
Arkansas	Indiana	Mississippi	North Dakota	Utah
California	Iowa	Missouri	Ohio	Vermont
Colorado	Kansas	Montana	Oklahoma	Virginia
Connecticut	Kentucky	Nebraska	Oregon	Washington
Delaware	Louisiana	Nevada	Pennsylvania	West Virginia
Florida	Maine	New Hampshire	Rhode Island	Wisconsin
Georgia	Maryland	New Jersey	South Carolina	Wyoming

Answers

Using an Atlas
Pages 4-5
Everglades; Florida; Denver; Colorado; Newport Beach; California; Tijuana
The adventure begins with a turn of the page!

United States
Page 7
1. AL; 2. AK; 3. AZ; 4. AR; 5. CA; 6. CO; 7. CT; 8. DE;
9. FL; 10. GA; 11. HI; 12. ID; 13. IL; 14. IN; 15. IA;
16. KS; 17. KY; 18. LA; 19. ME; 20. MD; 21. MA;
22. MI; 23. MN; 24. MS; 25. MO; 26. MT; 27. NE;
28. NV; 29. NH; 30. NJ; 31. NM; 32. NY; 33. NC;
34. ND; 35. OH; 36. OK; 37. OR; 38. PA; 39. RI;
40. SC; 41. SD; 42. TN; 43. TX; 44. UT; 45. VT;
46. VA; 47. WA; 48. WV; 49. WI; 50. WY

Alabama
Page 8
Huntsville, Alabama

Alaska
Page 9

```
K L L A F R E T A W M O
B A L D E A G L E S O A
S U Y L T R E E N L O N
R A E A T D L O G O S C
E E L S K N W I L M E H
E N G M O U N T A I N O
D U O T O T O A C K L R
N J A S K N T A I S S A
I O O W H A L E E E N G
E D O G S L E D R A C E
R A E B Y L Z Z I R G X
```

Arizona
Page 10
How deep?
$40 \div 10 = 4$ Empire State Buildings (up to 5,500 feet deep)
How long?
$191+60-10+17+19=277$ miles long (Utah is 270 miles wide)

Arkansas
Page 11 (clockwise from top left)
Fort Smith; Little Rock; Pine Bluff; El Dorado, Texarkana

California
Page 13
1. Reddingz; 2. Sequoia; 3. Joshua Tree;
4. Yosemite; 5. Kings Canyon; 6. Death Valley
State motto: "Eureka!"

Colorado
Page 14
B-5 Boulder; C-3 Rifle; A-3 Steamboat Springs;
B-6 Brush; A-2 Dinosaur National Monument;
A-6 Crow River; C-5 Castle Rock

Connecticut
Page 15 (Penguins)

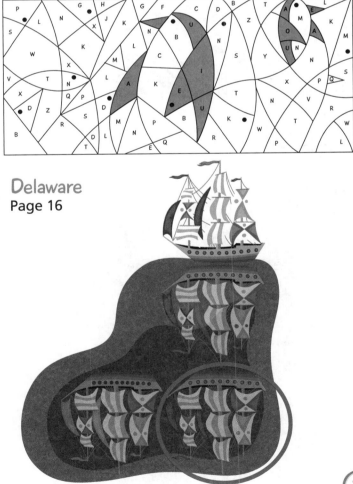

Delaware
Page 16

Answers

Florida
Page 17
OCEAN and CANOE; PALM and LAMP; PEARS and SPEAR; MELON and LEMON; TEN and NET; SHOE and HOSE; BEARD and BREAD

Georgia
Page 18

Hawaii
Page 19
Kilauea is an active volcano in Hawai'i Volcanoes National Park.

Idaho
Page 20

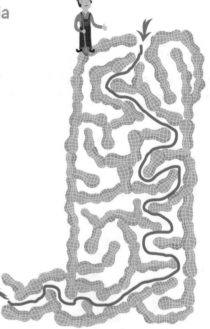

Illinois
Page 21
1. Paris; 2. Beardstown;
3. Sandwich; 4. Rock Falls;
5. Normal; 6. Champaign

Indiana
Page 22
1st – #2 orange; 2nd – #10 red; 3rd – #8 yellow

Iowa
Page 24

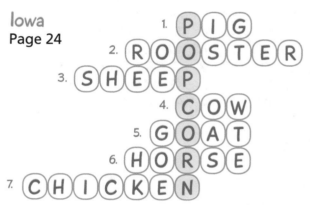

1. PIG
2. ROOSTER
3. SHEEP
4. COW
5. GOAT
6. HORSE
7. CHICKEN

More popcorn is produced in Sioux City, Iowa, than in any other place in the world.

Kansas
Page 25

Kentucky
Page 26
(B-4) Louisville; (B-5) Frankfort and Lawrenceburg;
(B-6) Lexington; (C-3) Owensville; (C-5) Danville;
(C-6) Richmond; (C-8) Pikeville; (D-3) Russellville;
(D-4) Bowling Green; (D-6) London & Williamsburg

Louisiana
Page 27

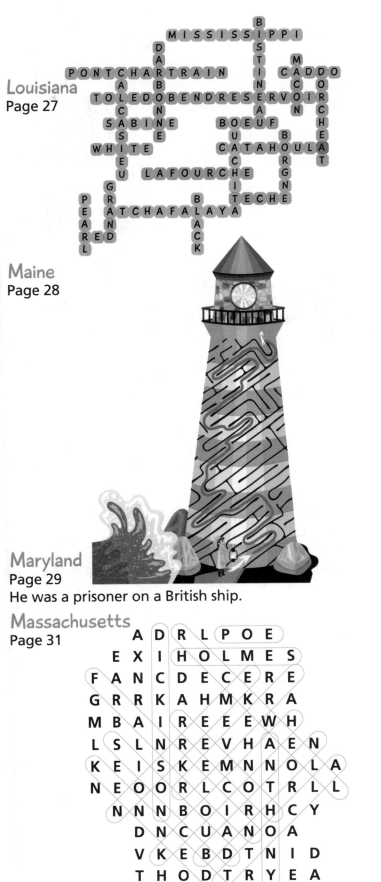

(crossword answers)
MISSISSIPPI, B, BISTINEAU, DARBONNE, PONTCHARTRAIN, CADDO, MACON, JACKSON, TOLEDO BEND RESERVOIR, DORCHEAT, SABINE, BOEUF, WHITE, SIEU, CATAHOULA, BUCTAHOULA, LAFOURCHE, GRAND, OUACHITA, BORGNE, TECHE, PEARL, GRAND RED, BLACK, ATCHAFALAYA

Maine
Page 28

Maryland
Page 29
He was a prisoner on a British ship.

Massachusetts
Page 31

```
      A  D  R  L  P  O  E
   E  X  I  H  O  L  M  E  S
F  A  N  C  D  E  C  E  R  E
G  R  R  K  A  H  M  K  R  A
M  B  A  I  R  E  E  E  W  H
L  S  L  N  R  E  V  H  A  E  N
K  E  I  S  K  E  M  N  N  O  L  A
N  E  O  O  R  L  C  O  T  R  L  L
   N  N  N  B  O  I  R  H  C  Y
      D  N  C  U  A  N  O  A
      V  K  E  B  D  T  N  I  D
      T  H  O  D  T  R  Y  E  A
   A  D  A  M  S  Y  U
```

Michigan
Page 32

 Standard

Minnesota
Page 33
Across: 3. Mille; 4. Vermilion; 6. Leech
Down: 1. Upper Red; 2. Winnibigoshish; 5. L. Itasca;
6. Lower Red

Mississippi
Page 34
paddlewheel, paddle, pail, palm tree, pants, park, park bench, parking meter, parrot, patch (eye), path, paw, pegleg, pelican, pencil, pepper, periscope, person, picnic, pier, pig, pillow, pineapple, pipe, pirate, plane, plate, pony, poodle, post, puddle

Missouri
Page 35

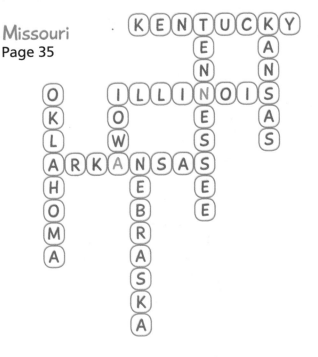

(crossword answers)
KENTUCKY, TENNESSEE, KANSAS, OKLAHOMA, IOWA, ILLINOIS, ARKANSAS, NEBRASKA

Answers

Montana
Page 36

Nebraska
Page 37

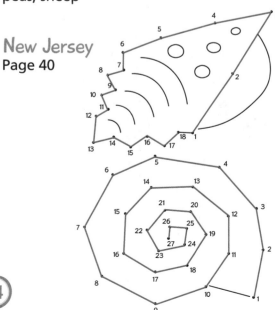

Nevada
Page 38
Las Vegas

New Hampshire
Page 39
ship, ramp, shrimp, man, pines, pear, pie, peas, sheep

New Jersey
Page 40

New Mexico
Page 41

New York
Page 43
mail box, periscope, sailboat on rock, snow boarder, candy cane, chimney on tent, fishing in fire, fire hydrant, dolphin in stream, shoe in tree

North Carolina
Page 44
frog, flashlight, fish, fin (on fish), flamingo, feather, fire or flame, fruit, flower, farmer, fan, flag, flippers, football, fork, foot/feet, face, forehead, fingers, fringe, frisbee (on towel or blanket), four (on flag), fence, funnel, floats, frankfurter

North Dakota
Page 45
1. Bowman; 2. Grand Forks; 3. Valley City;
4. Rugby; 5. Devil's Lake; 6. Carrington

Ohio
Page 47
Findlay, Newark, Ashland, Canton, Whitehall, Springfield, Logan, Athens, Portsmouth, Oxford, Fairborn, Middletown

Oklahoma

Page 48

dine — Enid: (B–5); bilead — Idabel (E–8); lowta — Lawton (E–5); wlassail — Sallisaw (C–8); leekomug — Okmulgee (C-7) ; moungy — Guymon (A–2); usalt — Tulsa (B–7); amimi — Miami (A–8); sheenwa — Shawnee (C–6); talliwerts — Stillwater (B–6)

Oregon

Page 49

Pennsylvania

Page 50

Rhode Island

Page 51

1. red light; 2. redwood; 3. red, white, and blue; 4. see red; 5. Little Red Riding Hood; 6. red carpet; 7. redhead

South Carolina

Page 52

South Dakota

Page 53

The correct order is P, E, O, P, L, E, which spells out PEOPLE

Tennessee

Page 54

Texas

Page 57

Answers

Utah
Page 58

T	G	R	P	P	H	B	L	S	T	I	Y	T
T	L	I	N	E	S	A	R	C	H	E	S	C
A	E	B	A	O	R	E	Z	Q	R	O	M	H
Z	N	N	T	P	D	I	N	O	S	A	U	R
R	C	O	U	L	E	N	N	B	K	I	R	I
O	A	O	R	E	F	G	S	G	N	T	A	S
L	N	T	A	O	E	X	D	O	Z	B	D	Q
N	Y	F	L	F	G	G	I	L	L	I	B	K
G	O	G	B	E	C	W	N	D	A	W	O	E
L	N	K	R	A	P	S	H	E	C	V	Y	N
A	S	T	I	R	D	O	U	N	H	R	R	D
D	D	A	D	T	E	N	D	S	B	O	C	R
E	T	E	G	H	V	P	L	P	A	I	H	A
N	X	R	E	O	Y	T	S	I	M	I	S	I
S	O	R	S	K	B	R	A	K	N	S	O	V
C	A	P	I	T	O	L	R	E	E	F	G	S
M	G	I	L	K	B	I	I	J	R	I	O	O
A	Q	R	L	E	B	S	H	O	A	O	N	G
O	J	C	R	A	Y	A	D	C	L	N	A	H
C	A	N	Y	O	N	L	A	N	D	S	P	C
T	A	H	H	R	N	I	M	L	A	W	M	I
R	C	A	L	E	X	S	Y	T	L	P	I	N
S	K	A	E	R	B	R	A	D	E	C	T	C

Vermont
Page 59
A = 7; B = 3; C = 1; X = 5
Fact number 5 is false.

Virginia
Page 60
Williamsburg

Washington
Page 62
Father's Day.

West Virginia
Page 63
1. Weirton; 2. Ohio; 3. Weston; 4. Potomac;
5. Harpers Ferry; 6. Tug Fork; 7. Kentucky;
8. Charleston
Fact: The New River is America's oldest river.

Wisconsin
Page 64
1. B; 2. A; 3. R; 4. A; 5. B; 6. O; 7. O (Baraboo)

Wyoming
Page 65

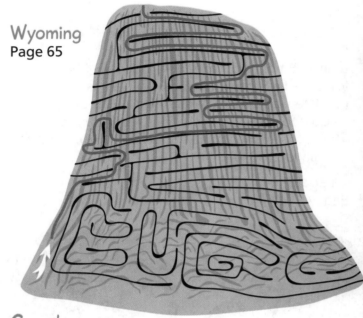

Canada
Page 67

Mexico
Page 68-69
1. Caribbean Sea; 2. Tijuana; 3. Tabasco;
4. Tortilla;5. Rio Grande; 6. Acapulco; 7. Mexicali;
8. Chihuahua; 9. Pacific Ocean; 10. Guatemala;
11. Ciudad Juárez; 12. El Paso; 13. Belize;
14. Hermosillo
"Mexicans were once known as the men of corn."

Populations are from the 2010 U.S. Census or other national censuses.